Study Guide for the Art Tests

▶   ▶   ▶   ▶   ▶   ▶   ▶   ▶   ▶   ▶   ▶   ▶

A PUBLICATION OF ETS

Table of Contents
Study Guide for the Art Tests

▶   ▶   ▶   ▶   ▶   ▶   ▶   ▶   ▶   ▶   ▶   ▶

The *Art: Content, Traditions, Aesthetics, and Criticism (Art CTAC)* Test

Chapter 1
Introduction to the Art Tests and Suggestions for Using This Study Guide

► ► ► ► ► ► ► ► ► ► ►

Introduction to the Art Tests

The Praxis Art tests are designed for individuals completing teacher training programs who plan to become teachers of art. ETS works in collaboration with teacher educators, higher education content specialists, and accomplished practicing teachers to keep the tests updated and representative of current standards.

The guide covers three different Art tests. One of them is multiple choice; that is, it presents questions with several possible answer choices, from which you must choose the best answer and indicate your response on an answer sheet. Other tests are constructed-response tests; that is, you are asked to answer a question or group of questions by writing out your response. It is not accurate to call constructed-response tests essay tests, because your response will not be graded on the basis of how it succeeds as an essay. Instead, your constructed response will be graded on the basis of how well it demonstrates an understanding of the principles of art and their appropriate applications.

This guide covers the following tests:

The *Art: Content Knowledge* test (0133) consists of 120 multiple-choice questions and covers three major areas, in the following proportions:

Content Category	Approximate Number of Questions	Approximate Percentage of Examination
I. Traditions in Art, Architecture, Design, and the Making of Artifacts	43	36%
II. Art Criticism and Aesthetics	30	25%
III. The Making of Art	47	39%

Test takers have two hours to complete the test.

The test is not intended to assess your teaching skills but rather your knowledge in the major areas of art history, criticism and aesthetics, and art making.

The *Art Making* test (0131) consists of two 5-minute constructed-response questions and two 25-minute constructed-response questions that cover two major areas, in the following proportions:

Content Category	Approximate Number of Questions	Approximate Percentage of Examination
I. Working Knowledge of Basic Art Concepts and Techniques of Art Making	2	24%
II. Documentation of Personal Art Making	2	76%

Test takers have one hour to complete the test.

The test is intended to assess your knowledge in the major areas of art making.

The *Art: Content, Traditions, Aesthetics, and Criticism* test (0132) consists of three constructed-response questions and covers three major areas, in the following proportions:

Content Category	Approximate Number of Questions	Approximate Percentage of Examination
I. The Content of Works of Art	1	33%
II. Global Traditions in Art, Architecture, and Design	1	33%
III. Criticism and Aesthetics	1	33%

Test takers have one hour to complete the test.

The test is intended to assess your knowledge in the major areas of art history, criticism, and aesthetics.

How to Use This Book

This book gives you instruction, practice, and test-taking tips to help you prepare for taking the Art tests. In chapter 2 you will find a discussion of The Praxis Series™—what it is and how the tests are developed. If you plan to take the *Art: Content Knowledge* test, you should turn to chapters 3, 4, 5, and 6 to review the topics likely to be covered on the test, get tips on succeeding at multiple-choice tests, work through practice questions, and see the answers to the practice questions, along with explanations of those answers. If you plan to take one or more constructed-response tests, you should turn to chapter 7 for information on how to succeed on this type of test. Then chapters 8, 9, and 10 (for the *Art Making* test) and 11, 12, and 13 (for the *Art: Content, Traditions, Aesthetics, and Criticism* test) will help you prepare for the test, work through practice questions, and see sample responses and how they were scored.

Where should you start? All users of this book will probably want to begin with the following two steps:

- **Become familiar with the test content.** Note what the appropriate chapter of the book says about the topics covered in the test you plan to take.

- **Consider how well you know the content in each subject area.** Perhaps you already know that you need to build your skills in a particular area. If you're not sure, skim over the chapters that cover test content to see what topics they cover. If you encounter material that feels unfamiliar or difficult, mark those pages to remind yourself to spend extra time in these sections.

Also, all users of this book will probably want to end with these two steps:

- **Familiarize yourself with test taking.** Chapter 3 is designed to answer frequently asked questions about multiple-choice tests, such as whether it is a good idea to guess on a test. Similarly, chapter 7 explains how constructed-response tests are scored and contains valuable tips on how to succeed on a test in this format. With either format, you can simulate the experience of the test by working through the practice questions within specified time limits. Choose a time and place where you will not be interrupted or distracted. After you complete the practice questions, use the appropriate chapter(s) to score your responses to the multiple-choice questions. Look over the explanations of the questions you missed and see whether you understand them and could answer similar questions correctly. The scoring key identifies which topic each question addresses, so you can see which areas are your strongest and weakest. Then plan any additional studying according to what you've learned about your understanding of the topics and your strong and weak areas. For the constructed-response questions, you can see sample responses that scored well, scored poorly, or scored in between. By examining these sample responses, you can focus on the aspects of your own practice responses that were successful and unsuccessful. This knowledge will help you plan any additional studying you might need.

- **Register for the test and consider last-minute tips.** Consult http://www.ets.org/praxis/index.html to learn how to register for the test. Also, review the checklist in chapter 14 to make sure you are ready for the test.

What you do between these first steps and these last steps depends on whether you intend to use this book to prepare on your own or as part of a class or study group.

Using this book to prepare on your own

If you are working by yourself to prepare for an Art test, you may find it helpful to fill out the Study Plan Sheet in appendix A. This worksheet will help you to focus on what topics you need to study most, identify materials that will help you study, and set a schedule for doing the studying.

Using this book as part of a study group

People who have a lot of studying to do sometimes find it helpful to form a study group with others who are preparing toward the same goal. Study groups give members opportunities to ask questions and get detailed answers. In a group, some members usually have a better understanding of certain topics, while others in the group may be better at other topics. As members take turns explaining concepts to each other, everyone builds self-confidence. If the group encounters a question that none of the members can answer well, the members can go as a group to a teacher or other expert and get answers efficiently. Because study groups schedule regular meetings, group members study in a more disciplined fashion. They also gain emotional support. The group should be large enough so various people can contribute various kinds of knowledge, but small enough that it stays focused. Often, three to six people is a good size.

Here are some ways to use this book as part of a study group:

- **Plan the group's study program.** Parts of the Study Plan Sheet in appendix A can help to structure your group's study program. By filling out the first five columns and sharing the work sheets, everyone will learn more about your group's mix of abilities and about the resources (such as textbooks) that members can share with the group. In the sixth column ("Dates planned for study of content"), you can create an overall schedule for your group's study program.

- **Plan individual group sessions.** At the end of each session, the group should decide what specific topics will be covered at the next meeting and who will present each topic. Use the topic headings and subheadings in the chapter that covers the topics for the test you will take.

- **Prepare your presentation for the group.** When it's your turn to be presenter, prepare something that's more than a lecture. Write five to ten original questions to pose to the group. Practicing writing actual questions can help you better understand the topics covered on the test as well as the types of questions you will encounter. It will also give other members of the group extra practice at answering questions.

- **Take the practice test together.** The idea of the practice questions is to simulate an actual administration of the test, so scheduling a test session with the group will add to the realism and will also help boost everyone's confidence.

- **Learn from the results of the practice questions.** For each test, use the corresponding chapter with the correct answers to score each other's answer sheets. Then plan one or more study sessions based on the questions that group members got wrong. For example, each group member might be responsible for a question that he or she got wrong and could use it as a model to create an original question to pose to the group, together with an explanation of the correct answer modeled after the explanations in this guide.

Whether you decide to study alone or with a group, remember that the best way to prepare is to have an organized plan. The plan should set goals based on specific topics and skills that you need to learn, and it should commit you to a realistic set of deadlines for meeting these goals. Then you need to discipline yourself to stick with your plan and accomplish your goals on schedule.

Note: Every effort is made to provide the most recent information in this study guide. However, The Praxis Series tests are continually evaluated and updated. You will always find the most recent information about these tests, including the topics covered, number of questions, time allotted, and scoring criteria, in the *Test at a Glance* materials available online at http://www.ets.org/praxis/prxtest.html.

Chapter 2
Background Information on The Praxis Series™ Subject Assessments

► ► ► ► ► ► ► ► ► ► ► ►

What Are The Praxis Series Subject Assessments?

The Praxis Series Subject Assessments are designed by ETS to assess your knowledge of specific subject areas. They are a part of the licensing procedure in many states. This study guide covers assessments that test your knowledge of the actual content you will be expected to teach once you are licensed. Your state has adopted The Praxis Series tests because it wants to confirm that you have achieved a specified level of mastery in your subject area before it grants you a license to teach in a classroom.

The Praxis Series tests are part of a national testing program, meaning that the tests covered in this guide are required in more than one state for licensure. The advantage of a national program is that if you want to move to another state, you can transfer your scores from one state to another. However, each state has specific test requirements and passing scores. If you are applying for a license in another state, you will want to verify the appropriate test and passing score requirements. This information is available online at www.ets.org/praxis/ or by calling ETS at 800-772-9476 or 609-771-7395.

What Is Licensure?

Licensure in any area—for example, medicine, law, architecture, accounting, cosmetology—is an assurance to the public that the person holding the license possesses sufficient knowledge and skills to perform important occupational activities safely and effectively. In the case of teacher licensing, a license tells the public that the individual has met predefined competency standards for beginning teaching practice.

Because a license makes such a serious claim about its holder, licensure tests are usually quite demanding. In some fields, licensure tests have more than one part and last for more than one day. Candidates for licensure in all fields plan intensive study as part of their professional preparation: some join study groups, others study alone. But preparing to take a licensure test is, in all cases, a professional activity. Because a licensure exam assesses the entire body of knowledge for the field you are entering, preparing for such a test takes planning, discipline, and sustained effort.

Why Does My State Require The Praxis Series Assessments?

Your state chose The Praxis Series Assessments because they assess the breadth and depth of content—called the "domain"—that your state wants its teachers to possess before they begin to teach. The level of content knowledge, reflected in the passing score, is based on recommendations of panels of teachers and teacher educators in each subject area. The state licensing agency and, in some states, the state legislature ratify the passing scores that have been recommended by panels of teachers.

What Do the Tests Measure?

The Praxis Series Subject Assessments are tests of content knowledge. They measure your understanding and skills in a particular subject area. Multiple-choice tests measure a broad range of knowledge across your content area. Constructed-response tests measure your ability to provide in-depth explanations of a few essential topics in a given subject area. Content-specific pedagogy tests, most of which are constructed response, measure your understanding of how to teach certain fundamental concepts in a subject area. The tests do not measure your actual teaching ability. However, they measure your knowledge of a subject and of how to teach it. The teachers in your field who help us design and write these tests, and the states that require them, do so in the belief that knowledge of your subject area is the first requirement for licensing. Teaching combines many complex skills, only some of which can be measured by a single test. While the tests covered in this study guide measure content knowledge, your teaching ability is a skill that is typically measured in other ways— for example, through observation, videotaped practice, or portfolios.

How Were These Tests Developed?

ETS began the development of The Praxis Series Subject Assessments with a survey. For each subject, teachers around the country in various teaching situations were asked to judge which knowledge and skills a beginning teacher in that subject needs to possess. Professors in schools of education who prepare teachers were asked the same questions. The responses were ranked in order of importance and sent out to hundreds of teachers for review. All of the responses to these surveys (called "job analysis surveys") were analyzed to summarize the judgments of these professionals. From their consensus, we developed guidelines, or specifications, for the multiple-choice and constructed-response tests. Each subject area had a committee of practicing teachers and teacher educators who wrote the specifications, which were reviewed and eventually approved by teachers. From the test specifications, groups of teachers and professional test developers created test questions that met content requirements and satisfied the *ETS Standards for Quality and Fairness.**

When your state adopted The Praxis Series Subject Assessments, local panels of practicing teachers and teacher educators in each subject area met to examine the tests and to evaluate each question for its relevance to beginning teachers in your state. This is called a "validity study" because local practicing teachers validate that the test content is relevant to the job. For the test to be adopted in your state, teachers in your state must judge that it is valid. During the validity study, the panel also provides a passing-score recommendation. This process includes a rigorous review to determine how many of the test questions a beginning teacher in that state would be able to answer correctly. Your state's licensing agency then reviewed the panel's recommendations and made a final determination of the passing-score requirement.

Throughout the development process, practitioners in the teaching field—teachers and teacher educators— participated in defining what The Praxis Series Subject Assessments would cover, which test would be used for licensure in your subject area, and what score would be needed to achieve licensure. This practice is consistent with how professional licensure works in most fields: those who are already licensed oversee the licensing of new practitioners. When you pass one of The Praxis Series Subject Assessments, you and the practitioners in your state will have evidence that you have the knowledge and skills required for beginning teaching practice.

---

* *ETS Standards for Quality and Fairness* (2003, Princeton, NJ) are consistent with the "Standards for Educational and Psychological Testing," industry standards issued jointly by the American Educational Research Association, the American Psychological Association, and the National Council on Measurement in Education (1999, Washington, DC).

Chapter 3

Succeeding on Multiple-Choice Questions

► ► ► ► ► ► ► ► ► ► ► ►

Understanding Multiple-Choice Questions

When you read multiple-choice questions on the Praxis *Art: Content Knowledge* test, you will probably notice that the syntax (word order) is different from the word order you're used to seeing in ordinary material that you read, such as newspapers or textbooks. One of the reasons for this difference is that many test questions contain the phrase "which of the following."

To answer a multiple-choice question successfully, you need to consider carefully the context set up by the question and limit your choice of answers to the list given. The purpose of the phrase "which of the following" is to remind you to do this. For example, look at this question.

Which of the following is a flavor made from beans?

(A) Strawberry
(B) Cherry
(C) Vanilla
(D) Mint

You may know that chocolate and coffee are also flavors made from beans, but they are not listed, and the question asks you to select from the list that follows ("which of the following"). So the answer has to be the only bean-derived flavor in the list: vanilla.

Notice that the answer can be substituted for the phrase "which of the following." In the question above, you could insert "vanilla" for "which of the following" and have the sentence "Vanilla is a flavor made from beans." Sometimes it helps to cross out "which of the following" and insert the various choices. You may want to give this technique a try as you answer various multiple-choice questions on the practice test.

Looking carefully at the "which of the following" phrase helps you to focus on what the question is asking you to find and on the answer choices. In the simple example above, all of the answer choices are flavors. Your job is to decide which flavor is the one made from beans.

The vanilla bean question is straightforward. But the phrase "which of the following" can also be found in more challenging questions. Look at this question:

Which of the following movements in twentieth-century art most closely shared the underlying concerns of Dada?

(A) Conceptual Art
(B) Fauvism
(C) Social Realism
(D) Cubism

The placement of "which of the following" tells you that the list of choices is a list of examples (in this case, examples of movements in twentieth-century art). What are you supposed to find as an answer? You are supposed to find the choice that most closely shared the underlying concerns of Dada.

ETS test developers and editors work very hard to word each question as clearly as possible. Sometimes, though, it helps to put the question in your own words. Here, you could paraphrase the question as "Which of these art movements is most closely related to Dada?" The correct answer is (A). (Dada embraced nonsense, intuitions, and irrationality. Conceptual Art is also concerned more with an idea than with an object.)

You may also find that it helps to circle or underline each of the critical details of the question in your test book so you don't miss any of them. It's only by looking at all parts of the question carefully that you will have all the information you need to answer it. Circle or underline the critical parts of what is being asked in this question.

Which of the following artists made significant contributions to the Harlem Renaissance?

(A)   Jacob Lawrence
(B)   Henry Ossawa Tanner
(C)   Betye Saar
(D)   Jean-Michel Basquiat

Here is one possible way you may have annotated the question:

Which of the following <u>artists</u> made significant contributions to the Harlem Renaissance ?

(A)   Jacob Lawrence
(B)   Henry Ossawa Tanner
(C)   Betye Saar
(D)   Jean-Michel Basquiat

After thinking about the question, you can probably see that you are being asked to look at a list of artists and decide which one made significant contributions to the Harlem Renaissance. The correct answer is (A). The important thing is understanding what the question is asking. With enough practice, you should be able to determine what any question is asking. Knowing the answer is, of course, a different matter, but you have to understand a question before you can answer it correctly.

Understanding Questions Containing "NOT," "LEAST," or "EXCEPT"

The words "NOT," "LEAST," and "EXCEPT" can make comprehension of test questions more difficult. Such questions ask you to select the choice that *doesn't* fit, that is different in some specified way from the other answer choices. You must be very careful with this question type because it's easy to forget that you're selecting the negative. This question type is used in situations in which there are several good solutions, or ways to approach something, but also a clearly wrong way. These words are always capitalized when they appear in The Praxis Series test questions, but they are easily (and frequently) overlooked.

For the following test question, determine what kind of answer you need and what the details of the question are.

Which of the following is NOT a term used to describe brush types?

(A)   Bright
(B)   Flat
(C)   Flexible
(D)   Filbert

You're looking for a word that is NOT used to describe brush types. (C) is the correct answer—all of the other choices *are* terms used to describe brush types.

> **TIP** It's easy to get confused while you're processing the information to answer a question with a NOT, LEAST, or EXCEPT in the question. If you treat the word "NOT," "LEAST," or "EXCEPT" as one of the details you must satisfy, you have a better chance of understanding what the question is asking.

Be Familiar with Multiple-Choice Question Types

You will probably see more than one question format on a multiple-choice test. Here are examples of some of the more common question formats.

1. Complete the statement

In this type of question, you are given an incomplete statement. You must select the choice that will make the completed statement correct.

The architectural style that is derived from ancient Greece and Rome and is evident in the Capitol building in Washington, D.C., is known as

(A)   Classical
(B)   Rococo
(C)   Neoclassical
(D)   Baroque

To check your answer, reread the question and add your answer choice at the end. Be sure that your choice best completes the sentence. The correct answer is (C).

2. Which of the following

This question type is discussed in detail in a previous section. The question contains the details that must be satisfied for a correct answer, and it uses "which of the following" to limit the choices to the four choices shown, as this example demonstrates:

Which of the following is a safe practice in the art studio?

(A) Using one's hands to wipe ink containing lead white from an etching plate
(B) Wearing goggles while operating a grinder or polishing wheel
(C) Sweeping up quantities of dry clay dust without dampening the floor
(D) Spraying paint in an air-locked space

The correct answer is (B).

3. Questions containing "NOT," "LEAST," "EXCEPT"

This question type is discussed at length above. It asks you to select the choice that doesn't fit.

4. Other formats

New formats are developed from time to time in order to find new ways of assessing knowledge with multiple-choice questions. If you see a format you are not familiar with, read the directions carefully. Then read and approach the question the way you would any other question, asking yourself what you are supposed to be looking for and what details are given in the question that help you find the answer.

Other Useful Facts about the Test

1. You can answer the questions in any order. You can go through the questions from beginning to end, as many test takers do, or you can create your own path. Perhaps you will want to answer questions in your strongest area of knowledge first and then move from your strengths to your weaker areas. There is no right or wrong way. Use the approach that works best for you.

2. There are no trick questions on the test. You don't have to find any hidden meanings or worry about trick wording. All the questions on the test ask about subject matter knowledge in a straightforward manner.

3. Don't worry about answer patterns. There is one myth that says that answers on multiple-choice tests follow patterns. Another myth is that there will never be more than two questions with the same lettered answer following each other. There is no truth to either of these myths. Select the answer you think is correct based on your knowledge of the subject.

4. There is no penalty for guessing. Your test score for multiple-choice questions is based on the number of correct answers you have. When you don't know the answer to a question, try to eliminate any obviously wrong answers and then guess at the correct one.

5. It's OK to write in your test book. You can work out problems on the pages of the book, make notes to yourself, mark questions you want to review later, or write anything at all. Your test book will be destroyed after you are finished with it, so use it in any way that is helpful to you. But make sure to mark your answers on the answer sheet.

Smart Tips for Taking the Test

1. Put your answers in the right "bubbles." It seems obvious, but be sure that you are filling in the answer bubble that corresponds to the question you are answering. A significant number of test takers fill in a bubble without checking to see that the number matches the question they are answering.

2. Skip the questions you find extremely difficult. There are sure to be some questions that you think are hard. Rather than trying to answer these on your first pass through the test, leave them blank and mark them in your test book so you can come back to them later. Pay attention to the time as you answer the rest of the questions on the test, and try to finish with 10 or 15 minutes remaining so that you can go back over the questions you left blank. Even if you don't know the answer the second time you read the questions, see if you can narrow down the possible answers, and then guess.

3. Keep track of the time. Take a watch to the test, in case the clock in the test room is difficult for you to see. You will probably have plenty of time to answer all the questions, but if you find yourself becoming bogged down in one section, you might decide to move on and go back to that section later.

4. Read all of the possible answers before selecting one—and then reread the question to be sure the answer you have selected really answers the question being asked. Remember that a question that contains a phrase such as "Which of the following does NOT..." is asking for the one answer that is NOT a correct statement or conclusion.

5. Check your answers. If you have extra time left over at the end of the test, look over each question and make sure that you have filled in the bubble on the answer sheet as you intended. Many test takers make careless mistakes that they could have corrected if they had checked their answers.

6. Don't worry about your score when you are taking the test. No one is expected to answer all the questions correctly. Your score on this test is *not* analogous to your score on the SAT, the GRE, or other similar-looking (but in fact very different!) tests. It doesn't matter on this test whether you score very high or barely pass. If you meet the minimum passing score for your state and you meet the state's other requirements for obtaining a teaching license, you will receive a license. In other words, your actual score doesn't matter, as long as it is above the minimum required score. With your score report you will receive a booklet entitled *Understanding Your Praxis Scores*, which lists the passing scores for your state.

Chapter 4

Study Topics for the *Art: Content Knowledge* Test

► ► ► ► ► ► ► ► ► ► ► ►

Introduction to the Test

The Art: Content Knowledge test is designed to measure the subject-area knowledge and competencies necessary for a beginning teacher of art. This test assumes that in addition to studying studio art, you have studied some art history during your college career, whether through a survey of art history course, through the incorporation of art history into other courses, or through more in-depth or specialized course work. The topics for questions are those that are typically covered in introductory courses for art majors. The questions are divided into three broad areas: Traditions in Art, Architecture, Design, and the Making of Artifacts; Art Criticism and Aesthetics; and the Making of Art. It is understood that college art history courses vary and that test takers' studio backgrounds also vary in their emphases. Thus, it is likely that different candidates will find different questions more or less difficult. The questions are all designed to focus on information that it would be reasonable to expect a beginning teacher to know. Some historical questions will require identification of major works of art, artists, or monuments, but the test as a whole includes many other kinds of questions, as outlined below.

This chapter is intended to help you organize your preparation for the test and to give you a clear indication about the depth and breadth of the knowledge required for success on the test.

You may find it helpful to refer to the bibliography on pages 60–62.

Here is an overview of the areas covered on the test, along with their subareas:

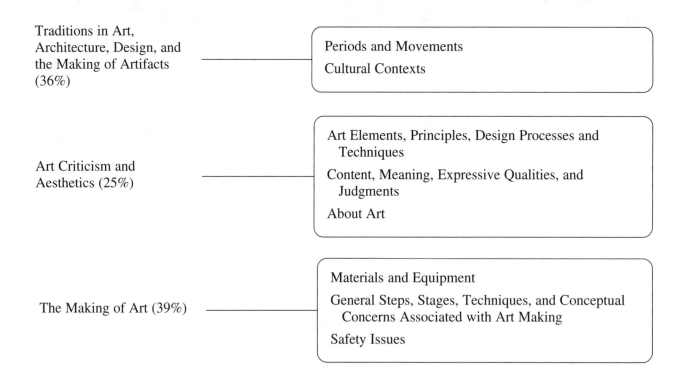

Traditions in Art, Architecture, Design, and the Making of Artifacts (36%)

- Periods and Movements
- Cultural Contexts

Art Criticism and Aesthetics (25%)

- Art Elements, Principles, Design Processes and Techniques
- Content, Meaning, Expressive Qualities, and Judgments
- About Art

The Making of Art (39%)

- Materials and Equipment
- General Steps, Stages, Techniques, and Conceptual Concerns Associated with Art Making
- Safety Issues

Using the topic lists that follow

Virtually all accredited undergraduate art programs address the majority of these topics. However, you are not expected to be an expert on all aspects of the topics that follow. You should understand the major characteristics of each topic and be able to relate it to appropriate works of art or aspects of art making.

For instance, here is one of the topic lists in "Art Elements, Principles, Design Processes and Techniques" under "Art Criticism and Aesthetics":

Art Elements, Principles, Design Processes and Techniques

- Vocabulary and concepts used in discussing the making of art and artifacts

- Vocabulary and concepts used in discussion of traditional art elements and principles of design (e.g., color, line, shape, unity, and balance) and the vocabulary and concepts used to discuss the strategies and techniques of contemporary art (e.g., juxtaposition, transformation, tension)

Referring to textbooks, state standards documents, or other sources as needed, make sure you can describe the art elements and principles of design in your own words. For example, you should be able to think to yourself that "Texture is …" or "Balance is …." It is also very important to be able to recognize how the art elements or principles of design function in a particular work of art.

You are likely to find that the topics below are covered by most introductory art history textbooks and textbooks for related fields (such as those devoted to specific areas of art or design, architecture, world cultures, and so on), but a general-survey textbook may not cover all the subtopics. Consult materials and resources, including lecture notes, from all your art course work. You should be able to match up specific topics and subtopics with what you have covered in your courses. In the case of the topics listed under "The Making of Art," much of your knowledge may come directly from studio classes.

Try not to be overwhelmed by the volume and scope of content knowledge in this guide. An overview such as this list of art topics does not offer you a great deal of context. Although a specific term, movement, or artist may not seem familiar as you see it here, you might find that you recognize it when it is applied to a specific work of art. Many of the items on the actual Praxis test will provide you with a context for these topics or terms, as you will see when you look at the practice questions in chapter 5.

Special questions marked with stars

Interspersed throughout the list of topics are questions that are outlined in boxes and preceded by stars (★). These questions are intended to help you test your knowledge of fundamental concepts and your ability to apply fundamental concepts to thinking about art. Most of the questions require you to combine several pieces of knowledge in order to focus your understanding and formulate an integrated response. If you spend time on these questions, you will gain increased understanding and facility with the subject matter covered on the test. You might want to discuss these questions and your answers with a teacher or mentor. Working with a friend can also be an effective way of preparing for the test.

Note that the questions marked with stars are not short answer or multiple choice and that this study guide does not provide the answers. The questions marked with stars are intended as study questions, not practice questions like those in chapter 5. Thinking about the answers to them should improve your understanding of fundamental concepts and will probably help you answer a broad range of questions on the test. For example, the following box with a star appears in the list of study topics under "Periods and Movements: Features that are characteristic of, or that originated in, widely known styles, periods, or movements."

> ★ How did the development of concrete affect ancient Roman architecture?

If you think about this question, perhaps jotting down some notes on methods of construction and materials used in large public structures such as the Pantheon, the Coliseum, and aqueducts, and how large structures function in the everyday life of a society, you will have probably prepared yourself to answer multiple-choice questions similar to the one below:

Classical Roman architecture differs from ancient Greek architecture in part because the development of the arch, the vault, and the dome enabled Roman architects to construct

(A) large interior spaces that were unobstructed by interior supports
(B) vast areas of wall that could accommodate murals
(C) civic buildings that were made of inexpensive materials
(D) public monuments that required a relatively small labor force

The development of quick-drying concrete and the use of wooden frames allowed the Romans to create vast open and unobstructed spaces covered by domes or barrel vaults that would accommodate large public gatherings. The common post-and-lintel construction method (vertical supports bearing horizontal beams) used by the Greeks required many columnar supports (hypostyle hall), thus limiting the creation of impressive open spaces. (A) is the correct answer.

Study Topics

Traditions in Art, Architecture, Design, and the Making of Artifacts

Periods and Movements

- Vocabulary and concepts used in discussing specific elements and dimensions of artworks, artifacts, and architecture created during various periods, styles, or movements

★ For major styles or movements (e.g., Greek temples, Gothic cathedrals, Renaissance painting), make a list of important characteristics and innovations and define terms used to describe the artworks.

- Artworks, artifacts, and architecture that are representative of widely known Western artists, styles, periods, or movements, identified through characteristic features or elements

★ Scan through a survey of art history text; when you look at reproductions of major works, what features or elements of the works enable you to identify them or the artists who made them?

- Artworks, artifacts, and architecture that are representative of non-Western cultures, identified through characteristic features or elements

★ What ritual or social purposes do works of art serve in cultures such as those of the Native Americans of the Southwest or the Pacific Northwest?

- Widely known artists, artworks, artifacts, or architecture

- Features that are characteristic of, or that originated in, widely known styles, periods, or movements

★ How did the development of concrete affect ancient Roman architecture?

Cultural Contexts

- Vocabulary and concepts used in discussing art forms and techniques of art making that are relevant to a particular cultural context

- The impact on artists, artworks, artifacts, and architecture of cultural and other factors, including

  ▶ Economic and political influences

  ▶ Technological developments

  ▶ The natural environment

★ How did the invention of photography affect the history of painting?

★ What are some of the European movements in art that were influenced by events leading up to the First World War and the war itself? How do they differ from each other?

- The relationship between society and those who make art or artifacts

---

★ How has the education of women changed art making in style and content since the nineteenth century?

- Stylistic and thematic influences of artists, architects, designers, traditions, and movements on one another; relationships among artists, architects, designers, traditions, and movements

---

★ Choose a well-known twentieth-century artist who inspired a school or group of followers. What characteristics of the first artist's work were imitated? What changes did followers make?

Art Criticism and Aesthetics

Art Elements, Principles, Design Processes and Techniques

- Vocabulary and concepts used in discussing the making of art and artifacts

---

★ What are some of the differences between panel painting, such as egg tempera, and oil painting?

- Vocabulary and concepts used in discussion of traditional art elements and principles of design (e.g., color, line, shape, unity, and balance) and the vocabulary and concepts used to discuss the strategies and techniques of contemporary art (e.g., juxtaposition, transformation, tension)

★ Choose one of the principles of design (unity, variety, balance, emphasis, contrast, proportion, scale, rhythm, figure-ground relationship); how is it used in a range of works, moving from representation into abstraction?

Content, Meaning, Expressive Qualities, and Judgments about Art

- The relationship between form and content in art

★ Choose one of the major themes in Western art or the art of another culture; what are some different ways in which that theme has been expressed over time or in different places?

- Interpretation of artworks, including recognition of narrative content, imagery, symbolism, and emotional impact

- Features, techniques, themes, etc., that link or distinguish two or more artworks or artifacts

- Basic vocabulary, principles, and approaches to art criticism, aesthetics, and art history

★ How have major critics influenced ideas and attitudes about art?

- Basic principles of art criticism that are used in describing, analyzing, interpreting, and evaluating artworks and artifacts

- Interpretation and evaluation of art criticism as applied to given artworks and artifacts

The Making of Art

Materials and Equipment

- Materials and equipment used in art making, with reference to the following:

  ▶ Two-dimensional art (may include electronic media)

  ▶ Three-dimensional art

★ What materials would generally be used in watercolor painting and oil painting? How do they differ?

★ What tools and materials are most commonly used in a range of media, such as ceramics, printmaking, and photography?

General Steps, Stages, Techniques, and Conceptual Concerns Associated with Art Making

- The general steps, stages, techniques, and conceptual concerns associated with art making, with reference to the following:

  ▶ Two-dimensional art (may include electronic media)

  ▶ Three-dimensional art

  ▶ Design

★ What are the general advantages of each of three basic ways of creating a three-dimensional work—additive processes, subtractive processes, and fabrication?

★ For the media that you have used in depth, review the steps and stages of generally known processes, techniques, and conceptual concerns.

★ For the media that you have *not* used in depth, what are the basic processes or techniques associated with them?

Safety Issues

- Safety issues related to art making, with reference to the following:

  ▶ Two-dimensional art

  ▶ Three-dimensional art

★ How can an artist figure out whether a particular material is toxic and, if so, whether it can be used safely?

Chapter 5
Practice Questions—*Art: Content Knowledge*

▶ ▶ ▶ ▶ ▶ ▶ ▶ ▶ ▶ ▶ ▶ ▶ ▶

Now that you have studied the content topics and have worked through strategies related to multiple-choice questions, you should answer the following practice questions. You will probably find it helpful to simulate actual testing conditions, giving yourself 70 minutes to work on the questions. You can cut out and use the answer sheet provided if you wish.

Keep in mind that the test you take at an actual administration will have different questions, although the proportion of questions in each area and major subarea will be approximately the same. You should not expect the percentage of questions you answer correctly in this practice test to be exactly the same as when you take the test at an actual administration, since numerous factors affect a person's performance in any given testing situation.

When you have finished the practice questions, you can score your answers and read the explanations of the best answer choices in chapter 6.

THE **PRAXIS**
S E R I E S
Professional Assessments for Beginning Teachers ®

TEST NAME:

Art: Content Knowledge

70 Practice Questions

Time—70 Minutes

(**Note:** At the official test administration, there will be 120 questions,
and you will be allowed 120 minutes to complete the test.)

DO NOT USE INK

Use only a pencil with soft black lead (No. 2 or HB) to complete this answer sheet.
Be sure to fill in completely the oval that corresponds to the proper letter or number.
Completely erase any errors or stray marks.

(ETS)

THE PRAXIS SERIES™

Answer Sheet C

PAGE 1

1. NAME

Enter your last name and first initial.
Omit spaces, hyphens, apostrophes, etc.

Last Name (first 6 letters)   F I

(A–Z ovals grid)

2.

YOUR NAME: (Print)

Last Name (Family or Surname)   First Name (Given)   M. I.

MAILING ADDRESS: (Print)

P.O. Box or Street Address   Apt. # (If any)

City   State or Province

Country   Zip or Postal Code

TELEPHONE NUMBER: ( )   Home   Business

SIGNATURE: **TEST DATE:**

3. DATE OF BIRTH

Month	Day
Jan.	
Feb.	
Mar.	
April	
May	
June	
July	
Aug.	
Sept.	
Oct.	
Nov.	
Dec.	

(Day ovals 0–9)

4. SOCIAL SECURITY NUMBER

(ovals 0–9)

5. CANDIDATE ID NUMBER

(ovals 0–9)

6. TEST CENTER / REPORTING LOCATION

Center Number   Room Number

Center Name

City   State or Province

Country

7. TEST CODE / FORM CODE

(ovals 0–9)

8. TEST BOOK SERIAL NUMBER

9. TEST FORM

10. TEST NAME

MH04167   Q2573-06   51055 • 08920 • TF74E400

202974

1 2 3 4

CERTIFICATION STATEMENT: (Please write the following statement below. DO NOT PRINT.)

"I hereby agree to the conditions set forth in the *Registration Bulletin* and certify that I am the person whose name and address appear on this answer sheet."

____

____

____

SIGNATURE: ______________________________ **DATE:** ______ / ______ / ______
Month Day Year

BE SURE EACH MARK IS DARK AND COMPLETELY FILLS THE INTENDED SPACE AS ILLUSTRATED HERE: ● .

1	Ⓐ Ⓑ Ⓒ Ⓓ	**41**	Ⓐ Ⓑ Ⓒ Ⓓ	**81**	Ⓐ Ⓑ Ⓒ Ⓓ	**121**	Ⓐ Ⓑ Ⓒ Ⓓ
2	Ⓐ Ⓑ Ⓒ Ⓓ	**42**	Ⓐ Ⓑ Ⓒ Ⓓ	**82**	Ⓐ Ⓑ Ⓒ Ⓓ	**122**	Ⓐ Ⓑ Ⓒ Ⓓ
3	Ⓐ Ⓑ Ⓒ Ⓓ	**43**	Ⓐ Ⓑ Ⓒ Ⓓ	**83**	Ⓐ Ⓑ Ⓒ Ⓓ	**123**	Ⓐ Ⓑ Ⓒ Ⓓ
4	Ⓐ Ⓑ Ⓒ Ⓓ	**44**	Ⓐ Ⓑ Ⓒ Ⓓ	**84**	Ⓐ Ⓑ Ⓒ Ⓓ	**124**	Ⓐ Ⓑ Ⓒ Ⓓ
5	Ⓐ Ⓑ Ⓒ Ⓓ	**45**	Ⓐ Ⓑ Ⓒ Ⓓ	**85**	Ⓐ Ⓑ Ⓒ Ⓓ	**125**	Ⓐ Ⓑ Ⓒ Ⓓ
6	Ⓐ Ⓑ Ⓒ Ⓓ	**46**	Ⓐ Ⓑ Ⓒ Ⓓ	**86**	Ⓐ Ⓑ Ⓒ Ⓓ	**126**	Ⓐ Ⓑ Ⓒ Ⓓ
7	Ⓐ Ⓑ Ⓒ Ⓓ	**47**	Ⓐ Ⓑ Ⓒ Ⓓ	**87**	Ⓐ Ⓑ Ⓒ Ⓓ	**127**	Ⓐ Ⓑ Ⓒ Ⓓ
8	Ⓐ Ⓑ Ⓒ Ⓓ	**48**	Ⓐ Ⓑ Ⓒ Ⓓ	**88**	Ⓐ Ⓑ Ⓒ Ⓓ	**128**	Ⓐ Ⓑ Ⓒ Ⓓ
9	Ⓐ Ⓑ Ⓒ Ⓓ	**49**	Ⓐ Ⓑ Ⓒ Ⓓ	**89**	Ⓐ Ⓑ Ⓒ Ⓓ	**129**	Ⓐ Ⓑ Ⓒ Ⓓ
10	Ⓐ Ⓑ Ⓒ Ⓓ	**50**	Ⓐ Ⓑ Ⓒ Ⓓ	**90**	Ⓐ Ⓑ Ⓒ Ⓓ	**130**	Ⓐ Ⓑ Ⓒ Ⓓ
11	Ⓐ Ⓑ Ⓒ Ⓓ	**51**	Ⓐ Ⓑ Ⓒ Ⓓ	**91**	Ⓐ Ⓑ Ⓒ Ⓓ	**131**	Ⓐ Ⓑ Ⓒ Ⓓ
12	Ⓐ Ⓑ Ⓒ Ⓓ	**52**	Ⓐ Ⓑ Ⓒ Ⓓ	**92**	Ⓐ Ⓑ Ⓒ Ⓓ	**132**	Ⓐ Ⓑ Ⓒ Ⓓ
13	Ⓐ Ⓑ Ⓒ Ⓓ	**53**	Ⓐ Ⓑ Ⓒ Ⓓ	**93**	Ⓐ Ⓑ Ⓒ Ⓓ	**133**	Ⓐ Ⓑ Ⓒ Ⓓ
14	Ⓐ Ⓑ Ⓒ Ⓓ	**54**	Ⓐ Ⓑ Ⓒ Ⓓ	**94**	Ⓐ Ⓑ Ⓒ Ⓓ	**134**	Ⓐ Ⓑ Ⓒ Ⓓ
15	Ⓐ Ⓑ Ⓒ Ⓓ	**55**	Ⓐ Ⓑ Ⓒ Ⓓ	**95**	Ⓐ Ⓑ Ⓒ Ⓓ	**135**	Ⓐ Ⓑ Ⓒ Ⓓ
16	Ⓐ Ⓑ Ⓒ Ⓓ	**56**	Ⓐ Ⓑ Ⓒ Ⓓ	**96**	Ⓐ Ⓑ Ⓒ Ⓓ	**136**	Ⓐ Ⓑ Ⓒ Ⓓ
17	Ⓐ Ⓑ Ⓒ Ⓓ	**57**	Ⓐ Ⓑ Ⓒ Ⓓ	**97**	Ⓐ Ⓑ Ⓒ Ⓓ	**137**	Ⓐ Ⓑ Ⓒ Ⓓ
18	Ⓐ Ⓑ Ⓒ Ⓓ	**58**	Ⓐ Ⓑ Ⓒ Ⓓ	**98**	Ⓐ Ⓑ Ⓒ Ⓓ	**138**	Ⓐ Ⓑ Ⓒ Ⓓ
19	Ⓐ Ⓑ Ⓒ Ⓓ	**59**	Ⓐ Ⓑ Ⓒ Ⓓ	**99**	Ⓐ Ⓑ Ⓒ Ⓓ	**139**	Ⓐ Ⓑ Ⓒ Ⓓ
20	Ⓐ Ⓑ Ⓒ Ⓓ	**60**	Ⓐ Ⓑ Ⓒ Ⓓ	**100**	Ⓐ Ⓑ Ⓒ Ⓓ	**140**	Ⓐ Ⓑ Ⓒ Ⓓ
21	Ⓐ Ⓑ Ⓒ Ⓓ	**61**	Ⓐ Ⓑ Ⓒ Ⓓ	**101**	Ⓐ Ⓑ Ⓒ Ⓓ	**141**	Ⓐ Ⓑ Ⓒ Ⓓ
22	Ⓐ Ⓑ Ⓒ Ⓓ	**62**	Ⓐ Ⓑ Ⓒ Ⓓ	**102**	Ⓐ Ⓑ Ⓒ Ⓓ	**142**	Ⓐ Ⓑ Ⓒ Ⓓ
23	Ⓐ Ⓑ Ⓒ Ⓓ	**63**	Ⓐ Ⓑ Ⓒ Ⓓ	**103**	Ⓐ Ⓑ Ⓒ Ⓓ	**143**	Ⓐ Ⓑ Ⓒ Ⓓ
24	Ⓐ Ⓑ Ⓒ Ⓓ	**64**	Ⓐ Ⓑ Ⓒ Ⓓ	**104**	Ⓐ Ⓑ Ⓒ Ⓓ	**144**	Ⓐ Ⓑ Ⓒ Ⓓ
25	Ⓐ Ⓑ Ⓒ Ⓓ	**65**	Ⓐ Ⓑ Ⓒ Ⓓ	**105**	Ⓐ Ⓑ Ⓒ Ⓓ	**145**	Ⓐ Ⓑ Ⓒ Ⓓ
26	Ⓐ Ⓑ Ⓒ Ⓓ	**66**	Ⓐ Ⓑ Ⓒ Ⓓ	**106**	Ⓐ Ⓑ Ⓒ Ⓓ	**146**	Ⓐ Ⓑ Ⓒ Ⓓ
27	Ⓐ Ⓑ Ⓒ Ⓓ	**67**	Ⓐ Ⓑ Ⓒ Ⓓ	**107**	Ⓐ Ⓑ Ⓒ Ⓓ	**147**	Ⓐ Ⓑ Ⓒ Ⓓ
28	Ⓐ Ⓑ Ⓒ Ⓓ	**68**	Ⓐ Ⓑ Ⓒ Ⓓ	**108**	Ⓐ Ⓑ Ⓒ Ⓓ	**148**	Ⓐ Ⓑ Ⓒ Ⓓ
29	Ⓐ Ⓑ Ⓒ Ⓓ	**69**	Ⓐ Ⓑ Ⓒ Ⓓ	**109**	Ⓐ Ⓑ Ⓒ Ⓓ	**149**	Ⓐ Ⓑ Ⓒ Ⓓ
30	Ⓐ Ⓑ Ⓒ Ⓓ	**70**	Ⓐ Ⓑ Ⓒ Ⓓ	**110**	Ⓐ Ⓑ Ⓒ Ⓓ	**150**	Ⓐ Ⓑ Ⓒ Ⓓ
31	Ⓐ Ⓑ Ⓒ Ⓓ	**71**	Ⓐ Ⓑ Ⓒ Ⓓ	**111**	Ⓐ Ⓑ Ⓒ Ⓓ	**151**	Ⓐ Ⓑ Ⓒ Ⓓ
32	Ⓐ Ⓑ Ⓒ Ⓓ	**72**	Ⓐ Ⓑ Ⓒ Ⓓ	**112**	Ⓐ Ⓑ Ⓒ Ⓓ	**152**	Ⓐ Ⓑ Ⓒ Ⓓ
33	Ⓐ Ⓑ Ⓒ Ⓓ	**73**	Ⓐ Ⓑ Ⓒ Ⓓ	**113**	Ⓐ Ⓑ Ⓒ Ⓓ	**153**	Ⓐ Ⓑ Ⓒ Ⓓ
34	Ⓐ Ⓑ Ⓒ Ⓓ	**74**	Ⓐ Ⓑ Ⓒ Ⓓ	**114**	Ⓐ Ⓑ Ⓒ Ⓓ	**154**	Ⓐ Ⓑ Ⓒ Ⓓ
35	Ⓐ Ⓑ Ⓒ Ⓓ	**75**	Ⓐ Ⓑ Ⓒ Ⓓ	**115**	Ⓐ Ⓑ Ⓒ Ⓓ	**155**	Ⓐ Ⓑ Ⓒ Ⓓ
36	Ⓐ Ⓑ Ⓒ Ⓓ	**76**	Ⓐ Ⓑ Ⓒ Ⓓ	**116**	Ⓐ Ⓑ Ⓒ Ⓓ	**156**	Ⓐ Ⓑ Ⓒ Ⓓ
37	Ⓐ Ⓑ Ⓒ Ⓓ	**77**	Ⓐ Ⓑ Ⓒ Ⓓ	**117**	Ⓐ Ⓑ Ⓒ Ⓓ	**157**	Ⓐ Ⓑ Ⓒ Ⓓ
38	Ⓐ Ⓑ Ⓒ Ⓓ	**78**	Ⓐ Ⓑ Ⓒ Ⓓ	**118**	Ⓐ Ⓑ Ⓒ Ⓓ	**158**	Ⓐ Ⓑ Ⓒ Ⓓ
39	Ⓐ Ⓑ Ⓒ Ⓓ	**79**	Ⓐ Ⓑ Ⓒ Ⓓ	**119**	Ⓐ Ⓑ Ⓒ Ⓓ	**159**	Ⓐ Ⓑ Ⓒ Ⓓ
40	Ⓐ Ⓑ Ⓒ Ⓓ	**80**	Ⓐ Ⓑ Ⓒ Ⓓ	**120**	Ⓐ Ⓑ Ⓒ Ⓓ	**160**	Ⓐ Ⓑ Ⓒ Ⓓ

FOR ETS USE ONLY	R1	R2	R3	R4	R5	R6	R7	R8	TR	CS

ART: CONTENT KNOWLEDGE

Time—70 Minutes
70 Questions

Directions: Each of the questions or incomplete statements below is accompanied by four suggested answers, completions, or visual images. Select the one that is best in each case and fill in the corresponding lettered space on the answer sheet with a heavy, dark mark so that you cannot see the letter. Some of the questions are based on artwork and visual images that appear in appendix C of this guide. The questions that have accompanying images in the appendix are signaled by boxed directions above each question.

TRADITIONS IN ART, ARCHITECTURE, DESIGN, AND THE MAKING OF ARTIFACTS

1. Which of the following artists' work is characterized by thickly applied paint and swirling brushstrokes?

   (A) Paul Gauguin
   (B) Vincent van Gogh
   (C) Edgar Degas
   (D) Claude Monet

2. The Spanish artist Pablo Picasso is most closely associated with which of the following artistic movements?

   (A) Abstract Expressionism
   (B) Constructivism
   (C) Fauvism
   (D) Cubism

3. Which of the following artists created mobiles as a sculptural avenue to explore "freedom of movement, the joy of ceaseless recombination of shapes"?

   (A) Henry Moore
   (B) Alexander Calder
   (C) Louise Nevelson
   (D) Barbara Hepworth

4. Strict geometry of form and a great simplicity of flat, planar colors characterize the best-known work of

   (A) Salvador Dali
   (B) Piet Mondrian
   (C) Wassily Kandinsky
   (D) Marcel Duchamp

5. The earliest known Greek drawings (before 800 B.C.) were recorded as geometric motifs on

   (A) paper
   (B) pottery
   (C) stone
   (D) temples

6. Egyptian art remained relatively stable over the centuries in large part because

   (A) little attention was paid to art in Egyptian society
   (B) art was seen as closely related to Egyptian ideas of an afterlife
   (C) Egyptian society presented few interesting subjects to depict
   (D) Egyptian artists lacked the technical skill to make innovations

7. Historically, Navajo artists are famous for their work with

   (A) silver and weaving
   (B) pottery and kachina dolls
   (C) birch bark and corn husk
   (D) beadwork and quill work

8. Which of the following is a clear example of post-and-lintel construction?

   (A) The Great Pyramids
   (B) Stonehenge
   (C) Rouen Cathedral
   (D) Notre-Dame-du-Haut

Questions 9 and 10 refer to the following image.

To answer the following questions please refer to the image as it is presented on page 171 in appendix C. The image is listed there under the same number as these questions.

9. This sculpture exhibits the figural quality known as

   (A) chiaroscuro
   (B) cloisonné
   (C) crenellation
   (D) contrapposto

10. The style of this work and its degree of naturalism identify it as having been made in

   (A) ancient Greece
   (B) ancient Rome
   (C) Renaissance Italy
   (D) eighteenth-century England

11. The formulation of a one-point perspective in drawing and painting during the Renaissance is credited to

   (A) Leonardo da Vinci
   (B) Leon Battista Alberti
   (C) Piero della Francesca
   (D) Filippo Brunelleschi

12. Many mosques, such as the Great Mosque at Cordoba, are characterized by which of the following?

   (A) An open, central space with an altar in the center
   (B) A large, flat area of wall space meant to absorb the decorative play of stained-glass windows
   (C) A huge portal with sculpted figures of saints and angels
   (D) A hypostyle hall topped by large horseshoe-shaped arches

13. Of the following, which is most characteristic of the church architecture of the Romanesque period of the Middle Ages?

   (A) Reliance on wood as the primary material for churches with high vaulted ceilings
   (B) Development of the flying buttress to lighten and open the nave walls
   (C) Use of both barrel- and groin-vaulted ceilings made of stone
   (D) Complete avoidance of any kind of sculptural ornament

14. The Battle of Hastings, which was significant in the Norman conquest of England, was portrayed in the

   (A) Bayeux Tapestry
   (B) Winchester Psalter
   (C) Book of Kells
   (D) Beatus manuscripts

Question 15 refers to the following image.

> To answer the following question, please refer
> to the image as it is presented on page 172 in
> appendix C. The image is listed there under the
> same number as this question.

15. The sculpture was made by

   (A) Ghiberti
   (B) Michelangelo
   (C) Donatello
   (D) Verrochio

---

16. The most consistent theme in the work of Pieter
    Bruegel the Elder was

   (A) idealized Flemish landscapes
   (B) portraits of local dignitaries
   (C) the life of the peasant
   (D) biblical subject matter

17. Eighteenth-century painter and graphic artist
    William Hogarth produced series of pictures that
    functioned chiefly as

   (A) social satire
   (B) landscape travel views
   (C) lessons from the Bible
   (D) historical narratives

18. A defining influence on Dutch Baroque art
    was the

   (A) insistence on religious subject matter
   (B) pressure to turn away from naturalism
   (C) rise of middle-class art consumers
   (D) influence of royal patronage

19. The style of El Greco's paintings can best be
    described as

   (A) Mannerist
   (B) Neoclassical
   (C) Rococo
   (D) High Renaissance

20. Goya's *Disasters of War* can be seen as the
    prototype for which of the following works by
    Pablo Picasso?

   (A) *Les Demoiselles d'Avignon*
   (B) *Guernica*
   (C) *Three Musicians*
   (D) *The Old Guitarist*

21. The Modernist art movement that glorified the
    machine by stating that "a speeding motorcar
    … is more beautiful than the *Nike of
    Samothrace*" was

   (A) Cubism
   (B) Futurism
   (C) Dadaism
   (D) Fauvism

22. Which of the following buildings is considered
    an Art Deco masterpiece?

   (A) Seagram Building, New York
   (B) Chrysler Building, New York
   (C) Johnson Wax Building, Racine,
       Wisconsin
   (D) Tribune Building, Chicago

23. Which of the following is an ancient technique
    that was revived by Mexican painters of the
    early twentieth century, such as Diego Rivera
    and José Clemente Orozco?

   (A) Stained glass
   (B) Fresco
   (C) Encaustic
   (D) Mosaic

24. Large-scale public works of art such as *Running
    Fence* and *Wrapped Reichstag* were created by

   (A) Doug and Mike Starn
   (B) Claes and Coosje Oldenburg
   (C) Nicola and Giovanni Pisano
   (D) Jeanne-Claude and Christo

ART CRITICISM AND AESTHETICS

25. When a painting is described as "painterly," it indicates that the artist has used the paint

    (A) in a very precise, controlled manner
    (B) with subtle shifts in value and color
    (C) in a loose, gestural way
    (D) with no evidence of brushstroke

Question 26 refers to the following image.

> To answer the following question, please refer to the image as it is presented on page 173 in appendix C. The image is listed there under the same number as this question.

26. Which of the following design principles is exemplified by this work?

    (A) Contrast
    (B) Figure-ground relationship
    (C) Proportion
    (D) Repetition

27. The paintings of Paul Cézanne reflect the artist's interest in which of the following?

    (A) The use of ambiguous, swirling space to create emotional effects
    (B) The relationship between spirituality and art
    (C) The analytic use of line, plane, and color to construct visual space
    (D) The incorporation of collage elements with traditional subjects

28. Titian's oil-painting method involved

    (A) multiple glazes of colors
    (B) an *alla prima* style of applying thick paint
    (C) scratching through paint to expose the canvas
    (D) a waxy medium known as encaustic

29. The term "picture plane" refers to which of the following?

    (A) The use of negative space around the subject of an artwork
    (B) The use of scale to organize the parts of an artwork
    (C) The flat surface on which an illusion of space is created
    (D) The embellishment of an object's surfaces with pictorial decoration

30. Negative areas in a work of art are best defined as which of the following?

    (A) The area that is occupied by a recognizable object
    (B) The area that constitutes the foreground of a work
    (C) The area that contains the least amount of detail
    (D) The area that is unoccupied by an object

31. Which of the following is considered a "plastic art"?

    (A) Sculpture
    (B) Painting
    (C) Photography
    (D) Printmaking

Questions 32 and 33 refer to the following image.

To answer the following questions, please refer to the image as it is presented on page 174 in appendix C. The image is listed there under the same numbers as these questions.

32. At the time this building was constructed, which of the following architectural features was an innovation that contributed to its spacious, well-lighted interior?

    (A) Pointed arches
    (B) Cross vaulting
    (C) Clerestory windows
    (D) Flying buttresses

33. Although this building style's "new light" and elegance sparked a range of responses, the prevailing view during this period came to be that physical beauty

    (A) was spiritually uplifting
    (B) distracted the faithful from prayers
    (C) inspired the sin of pride
    (D) was illustrative of biblical stories

34. Judy Chicago's *Dinner Party* celebrates

    (A) traditional family values, with an emphasis on motherhood
    (B) the first Thanksgiving celebrated by the Pilgrims
    (C) the role of women as food providers
    (D) the achievements and contributions of women throughout history

35. In Chinese art, dragons generally symbolize

    (A) evil magic
    (B) cunning strategy
    (C) good fortune and power
    (D) dreams and fantasy

36. Which of the following artists' work falls under the category of assemblage?

    (A) Louise Nevelson
    (B) Cindy Sherman
    (C) Dorothea Lange
    (D) Berthe Morisot

Question 37 refers to the following image.

To answer the following question, please refer to the image as it is presented on page 175 in appendix C. The image is listed there under the same number as this question.

37. Andrea Mantegna's ceiling painting in the Room of the Newlyweds illustrates the Renaissance technique of

    (A) trompe l'oeil
    (B) découpage
    (C) grisaille
    (D) frottage

38. The aesthetic theory known as formalism places an emphasis in artwork on

    (A) emotional qualities
    (B) realistic representation
    (C) design qualities
    (D) physical beauty

Questions 39 and 40 refer to the following image.

To answer the following questions, please refer to the image as it is presented on page 176 in appendix C. The image is listed there under the same numbers as these questions.

39. The medium of this work is

  (A) lithography
  (B) engraving
  (C) woodcut
  (D) silk screen

40. Painters like Vincent van Gogh, Edgar Degas, and Mary Cassatt all used this picture's method of

  (A) eliminating a middle ground in the composition
  (B) placing the horizon line low in the composition
  (C) creating a narrative with action stopped at a climactic point
  (D) highlighting large areas with white

41. Caravaggio's method of creating dramatic contrasts of dark and light, which influenced artists throughout Europe during the Baroque period, is called

  (A) grisaille
  (B) sfumato
  (C) tenebrism
  (D) contrapposto

42. Which of the following terms refers to the intensity of a color?

  (A) Hue
  (B) Saturation
  (C) Value
  (D) Luminosity

43. A sculptural form, often used by ancient Greeks to decorate temples, that protrudes significantly from a flat surface is known as a

  (A) plinth
  (B) high relief
  (C) fabrication
  (D) pediment

ART MAKING

44. Of the following, which designation represents the softest graphite compression for a pencil?

    (A) 3B
    (B) 6B
    (C) 3H
    (D) 6H

45. The most common solvent used in studio processes is

    (A) turpentine
    (B) polymer
    (C) alcohol
    (D) water

46. Which of the following is a drawing process that uses changes in value to represent a three-dimensional surface?

    (A) Simulation
    (B) Cross contour
    (C) Modeling
    (D) Linear perspective

47. Which of the following terms refers to the liquid that holds pigment in suspension?

    (A) Base
    (B) Vehicle
    (C) Solvent
    (D) Extender

48. Papier-mâché is best described as which of the following?

    (A) A process of gluing multiple layers of paper onto an armature
    (B) A process of casting wet paper into a mold to form a relief
    (C) A subtractive sculptural process that allows for fine detail
    (D) A method of casting polyresin objects

49. Which of the following types of tape is most commonly used in hard-edge painting?

    (A) Cellophane tape
    (B) Double-sided tape
    (C) Masking tape
    (D) Paper tape

50. Which of the following pairs of terms refers to hand-building processes with clay?

    (A) Coil..slab
    (B) Bisque..glaze
    (C) Extruded..wedged
    (D) Thrown..cast

51. Applying paint in a thick application is known as

    (A) impasto
    (B) contrapposto
    (C) sfumato
    (D) chiaroscuro

52. Chromatic gray can be achieved by mixing

    (A) black and white
    (B) orange and blue
    (C) red and purple
    (D) beige and gray

53. The term "aperture" in photography refers to

    (A) clarity
    (B) magnification
    (C) shutter speed
    (D) lens opening

54. Which of the following is NOT used in pen-and-ink drawing?

    (A) Quill
    (B) Stump
    (C) Nib
    (D) Penholder

55. In a two-dimensional work of art, a bird's-eye or worm's-eye view of an object can best be achieved by using which of the following perspectives?

    (A) Atmospheric
    (B) One-point
    (C) Two-point
    (D) Three-point

56. Which of the following is a pair of tools that is commonly used in printmaking?

    (A) Burin..squeegee
    (B) Ribbon tool..wire cutter
    (C) Pyrometer..cone
    (D) Tjanting..wax

57. In digital photography, image sharpness is determined by

    (A) reticulation
    (B) resolution
    (C) f-stop
    (D) shutter speed

58. Which of the following is the process in which fine metal wire is used to organize colors that are fused into hard enamel-like surfaces?

    (A) Encaustic
    (B) Glazing
    (C) Cloisonné
    (D) Engobe

59. Of the following, the ceramic clay that requires the highest firing temperature to mature is

    (A) terra cotta
    (B) stoneware
    (C) raku
    (D) true porcelain

60. When digital artwork is being prepared for printing, the color mode must be

    (A) RGB
    (B) duotone
    (C) TIFF
    (D) CMYK

61. Which of the following is a technique that involves brushing paint over a dried layer of paint so that the dried layer shows through?

    (A) Sizing
    (B) Stumping
    (C) Scumbling
    (D) Scruffing

62. Which of the following presents a significant health risk for absorption through healthy, unbroken skin?

    (A) Turpentine
    (B) Linseed oil
    (C) Gouache
    (D) White glue

63. The printmaking process that uses ink passing through a screen is

    (A) serigraphy
    (B) lithography
    (C) intaglio
    (D) etching

64. The term "lost-wax" refers to

    (A) the use of encaustic wax as a medium in painting
    (B) the use of melted paraffin as a resist medium in ceramic decoration
    (C) a technique of casting metal in a plaster mold
    (D) a step in developing an image on fabric in batik making

65. Work with which of the following requires good ventilation?

    (A) Graphite pencil
    (B) Wax resist
    (C) Acrylic painting
    (D) Etching bath

66. In computer-art paint programs, images are stored as pixels, a series of tiny dots called

    (A) an analog system
    (B) microprocessors
    (C) a digital system
    (D) bitmaps

67. Which of the following materials is used to stop paper from absorbing paint in water-based painting?

    (A) Frisket
    (B) Extender
    (C) Gesso
    (D) Gum

Question 68 refers to the following image.

To answer the following question, please refer to the image as it is presented on page 177 in appendix C. The image is listed there under the same number as this question.

68. Which of the following drawing processes is used to produce tonal values in this artwork?

    (A) Gesture
    (B) Stippling
    (C) Hatching
    (D) Contour

69. Which of the following printmaking processes is additive?

    (A) Lithography
    (B) Collagraphy
    (C) Stenciling
    (D) Intaglio

70. Which of the following terms refers to a printmaker's hand-inking roller?

    (A) Rocker
    (B) Burnisher
    (C) Scrim
    (D) Brayer

Chapter 6

Right Answers and Explanations—*Art: Content Knowledge*

► ► ► ► ► ► ► ► ► ► ► ►

Now that you have answered all of the practice questions for the *Art: Content Knowledge* test, you can check your work. Compare your answers to the multiple-choice questions with the correct answers in the table below.

Question Number	Correct Answer	Content Category	Question Number	Correct Answer	Content Category
1	B	Traditions in Art, Architecture, Design, and the Making of Artifacts	21	B	Traditions in Art, Architecture, Design, and the Making of Artifacts
2	D	Traditions in Art, Architecture, Design, and the Making of Artifacts	22	B	Traditions in Art, Architecture, Design, and the Making of Artifacts
3	B	Traditions in Art, Architecture, Design, and the Making of Artifacts	23	B	Traditions in Art, Architecture, Design, and the Making of Artifacts
4	B	Traditions in Art, Architecture, Design, and the Making of Artifacts	24	D	Traditions in Art, Architecture, Design, and the Making of Artifacts
5	B	Traditions in Art, Architecture, Design, and the Making of Artifacts	25	C	Art Criticism and Aesthetics
6	B	Traditions in Art, Architecture, Design, and the Making of Artifacts	26	D	Art Criticism and Aesthetics
7	A	Traditions in Art, Architecture, Design, and the Making of Artifacts	27	C	Art Criticism and Aesthetics
8	B	Traditions in Art, Architecture, Design, and the Making of Artifacts	28	A	Art Criticism and Aesthetics
9	D	Traditions in Art, Architecture, Design, and the Making of Artifacts	29	C	Art Criticism and Aesthetics
10	B	Traditions in Art, Architecture, Design, and the Making of Artifacts	30	D	Art Criticism and Aesthetics
11	D	Traditions in Art, Architecture, Design, and the Making of Artifacts	31	A	Art Criticism and Aesthetics
12	D	Traditions in Art, Architecture, Design, and the Making of Artifacts	32	D	Art Criticism and Aesthetics
13	C	Traditions in Art, Architecture, Design, and the Making of Artifacts	33	A	Art Criticism and Aesthetics
14	A	Traditions in Art, Architecture, Design, and the Making of Artifacts	34	D	Art Criticism and Aesthetics
15	C	Traditions in Art, Architecture, Design, and the Making of Artifacts	35	C	Art Criticism and Aesthetics
16	C	Traditions in Art, Architecture, Design, and the Making of Artifacts	36	A	Art Criticism and Aesthetics
17	A	Traditions in Art, Architecture, Design, and the Making of Artifacts	37	A	Art Criticism and Aesthetics
18	C	Traditions in Art, Architecture, Design, and the Making of Artifacts	38	C	Art Criticism and Aesthetics
19	A	Traditions in Art, Architecture, Design, and the Making of Artifacts	39	C	Art Criticism and Aesthetics
20	B	Traditions in Art, Architecture, Design, and the Making of Artifacts	40	A	Art Criticism and Aesthetics
			41	C	Art Criticism and Aesthetics
			42	B	Art Criticism and Aesthetics
			43	B	Art Criticism and Aesthetics
			44	B	The Making of Art
			45	D	The Making of Art
			46	C	The Making of Art
			47	B	The Making of Art
			48	A	The Making of Art
			49	C	The Making of Art
			50	A	The Making of Art
			51	A	The Making of Art
			52	B	The Making of Art
			53	D	The Making of Art
			54	B	The Making of Art

Question Number	Correct Answer	Content Category	Question Number	Correct Answer	Content Category
55	D	The Making of Art	63	A	The Making of Art
56	A	The Making of Art	64	C	The Making of Art
57	B	The Making of Art	65	D	The Making of Art
58	C	The Making of Art	66	D	The Making of Art
59	D	The Making of Art	67	A	The Making of Art
60	D	The Making of Art	68	B	The Making of Art
61	C	The Making of Art	69	B	The Making of Art
62	A	The Making of Art	70	D	The Making of Art

Explanations of Right Answers

1. The expressive brushstrokes of thick, vigorously applied paint, called impasto, is characteristic of the work of Vincent van Gogh. The correct answer, therefore, is (B).

2. The revolutionary style of painting first explored by Georges Braque and Pablo Picasso in 1907, which subsequently became a movement of broad international scope, is Cubism. The correct answer, therefore, is (D).

3. The signature works of Alexander Calder, the inventor of the mobile, are hanging mobiles set into motion by air currents and standing motorized "stabiles." Using diverse materials for the free-form shapes, Calder often worked on a monumental scale and considered his work "four dimensional drawings." The correct answer, therefore, is (B).

4. The Dutch painter Piet Mondrian evolved his abstract style of painting into a new rigorous geometric style he called Neoplasticism. In this style he limited himself to straight lines and basic colors to create art of great clarity and discipline. The correct answer, therefore, is (B).

5. During the "geometric period" in the ninth century B.C., Athens was the center for pottery production in ancient Greece. Notable vases decorated in geometric motifs were recovered there from the Dipylon cemetery. The correct answer, therefore, is (B).

6. For the Egyptians, art was associated with religious tradition and influenced by magic and a faith in transcendental forces. The correct answer, therefore, is (B).

7. The Navajo people of northern New Mexico and Arizona are best known for their silversmithing and rug weaving. The correct answer, therefore, is (A).

8. A "lintel" is a flat beam that spans posts; the stone construction at Stonehenge is a clear application of this system. None of the buildings mentioned in the other choices employs this construction system. The correct answer, therefore, is (B).

9. In this marble statue of Augustus from Prima Porta, dating to around 17 B.C., the body weight is borne mainly on one leg in a figural pose known as contrapposto. The correct answer, therefore, is (D).

10. This statue exhibits the ancient Roman preference for specific detail in portraiture in which capturing the actual features of the emperor was important. The correct answer, therefore, is (B).

11. A pioneer of perspective, Filippo Brunelleschi in 1413 produced pictures in which he used a single vanishing point (one-point perspective) to represent depth. The correct answer, therefore, is (D).

12. Many traditional Islamic mosques, such as the Great Mosque at Cordoba, are notable for a large hall called a hypostyle hall, in which the roof is supported by several rows of columns topped by large horseshoe-shaped arches. The correct answer, therefore, is (D).

13. The use of barrel vaults and groin vaults made of stone is characteristic of Romanesque architecture. Stone, not wood, was the primary material used; flying buttresses were introduced during the Gothic period; and sculpture was integrated into Romanesque churches. The correct answer, therefore, is (C).

14. Commissioned by Odo, Bishop of Bayeux, in 1070, the Bayeux Tapestry is a 20-inch-high, almost 230-foot-long pictorial narrative of William the Conqueror's conquest of England. The correct answer, therefore, is (A).

15. The reproduction is of Donatello's *David*; the correct answer is therefore (C).

16. Although he spent his career in major cities rather than in the countryside, Pieter Bruegel the Elder is most noted for his paintings of peasants and scenes of village life. The correct answer, therefore, is (C).

17. William Hogarth examined the mores and activities of the social and economic classes in his satirical "moral works," which were painted and then later engraved. In *A Harlot's Progress* (1732) he shows the downward spiral in the life of a prostitute. *A Rake's Progress* (1735) looks at the newly prosperous middle class, and *Marriage a la Mode* (1743) portrays upper-middle-class society. The correct answer, therefore, is (A).

18. In the seventeenth century, it was the "burghers," or the cities' merchant middle class, who cried out for works that glorified their own everyday life. For the first time in history, art became available to this new class of consumer. The correct answer, therefore, is (C).

19. El Greco employed the Mannerist conventions of portraying elongated figures in strained poses and using strong artificial color. Also typical of Mannerism, El Greco's work was intensely spiritual, emotional, and restless. The correct answer, therefore, is (A).

20. Both Goya's *Disasters of War* and Picasso's *Guernica* are passionate expressions of anguish at the brutality of war. None of the other Picasso works mentioned is related to war. The correct answer, therefore, is (B).

21. Futurism, which began in Italy in 1909, brought to art the force of motion and the noise and power of machinery. The Futurists issued several manifestos putting forth the idea of adding mechanized movement to the Cubist ideals of showing multiple points of view. The correct answer, therefore, is (B).

22. Architect William Van Alen's Chrysler Building, erected in 1930, is an archetypical American Art Deco skyscraper. The characteristics of its design, from the style of the mural and the ornate lobby to the radiating curves mimicking giant sunbeams on the building's dome, are decidedly Art Deco masterpieces. The correct answer, therefore, is (B).

23. In 1920 the new revolutionary Mexican government launched a program to inspire social change through art. Public walls were painted with frescoes glorifying Mexican history and culture. Diego Rivera and José Clemente Orozco were two major artists involved in this effort. The correct answer, therefore, is (B).

24. *Running Fence*, an 18-foot-high, 24½-mile-long line of white fabric across the landscape of northern California, and *Wrapped Reichstag*, the draping of the Berlin Reichstag in over 60 tons of silvery fabric held in place by 10 miles of blue rope, were the creations of husband-and-wife artists Jeanne-Claude and Christo. The correct answer, therefore, is (D).

25. Describing a work as "painterly" implies that it contains a departure from strict realism and has the appearance of a painting (as opposed to a drawing or photograph) in terms of loose, gestural uses of color and texture. Painterly works have brushstrokes that are clearly visible. The correct answer, therefore, is (C).

26. Repetition is the visual key that ties this piece together, unifies it, and controls the viewer's eye. As evident in this piece, *Repetition Nineteen I*, artist Eva Hesse often created elaborate, handmade pieces involving obsessive repetition. The correct answer, therefore, is (D).

27. Paul Cezanne was interested in structural analysis and the combination of formal grandeur (of the Old Masters) with contemporary color (Postimpressionism). His paintings are analytical in their use of line, plane, and color. The correct answer, therefore, is (C).

28. Titian worked in oil paint on canvas in a technique called glazing, in which thin layers of paint are painted over existing layers to build subtle color. Leaving the colors unblended, Titian hoped that the viewer's eye would instinctively blend them. The correct answer, therefore, is (A).

29. The flat surface of a picture on which an illusion of space is created is a picture plane. The correct answer, therefore, is (C).

30. The space around an object in a picture that is not occupied by the object is called the negative space or area. The correct answer, therefore, is (D).

31. Three-dimensional art, such as stone sculpture and modeling clay, is called "plastic art." The correct answer, therefore, is (A).

32. Flying buttresses relieve the wall by sending the thrust of the vault to the ground by way of a support that stands outside. As a result, the interior is larger and lighter in construction and can hold a greater proportion of windows. The correct answer, therefore, is (D).

33. The oldest aesthetic dictate, "All that which exists is light," is echoed in the Chartres Cathedral. The physical beauty and elaboration of the ornamentation, as well as the soaring upward construction, came to be viewed as spiritually uplifting. The correct answer, therefore, is (A).

34. Celebrating the achievements of women throughout history, the "table" created for Judy Chicago's *Dinner Party* is set with 39 place settings, each dedicated to an important woman (e.g., O'Keeffe, Susan B. Anthony, Sojourner Truth); the names of 999 additional "women of achievement" are inscribed on the floor of the piece. The correct answer, therefore, is (D).

35. The fabulous serpents in Chinese art, the dragons, generally symbolize good fortune and power. The correct answer, therefore, is (C).

36. Louise Nevelson is internationally known for her "sculptured walls," assemblages made of many boxes and compartments into which abstract shapes are assembled together with other commonplace "found objects." The correct answer, therefore, is (A).

37. When painted architecture appears to extend the real space of a room, it is called quadratura and is a form of trompe l'oeil. In the ceiling painting for the Room of the Newlyweds, Andrea Mantegna's illusion appears to extend the real architecture of the room into an imaginary space. The correct answer, therefore, is (A).

38. Formalism describes the formal design qualities of the work, such as line, shape and color. The correct answer, therefore, is (C).

39. The *Great Wave off Kanagawa* is a woodcut print, part of a series, *Thirty-six Views of Mt. Fuji* (1831), by the prominent woodblock artist Katsushika Hokusai. The correct answer, therefore, is (C).

40. One of the qualities of woodblock prints, as seen in *Great Wave off Kanagawa*, that influenced the French Impressionists was the patternistic flat quality of the colors. Also noted by the Impressionists were the work's off-center composition, flat planes, and radical cropping. The correct answer, therefore, is (A).

41. Tenebrism, from the Latin *tenebrae*, meaning "darkness," is the use of large, predominantly dark areas in a painting and is often used to describe the work of Caravaggio and his followers. The correct answer, therefore, is (C).

42. The degree of brilliance, intensity, and purity of a hue (the name of a particular color) is called the saturation. The correct answer, therefore, is (B).

43. A sculpture that projects from the background surface rather than standing freely is a relief. The degree of the projection is referred to as high, medium, or low. Ancient Greek temples are decorated with high-relief sculptures. The correct answer, therefore, is (B).

44. The core of a pencil is a compressed mixture of graphite and clay binder. Hard pencils contain a higher proportion of binder and are labeled with the letter H. Soft pencils contain a higher proportion of graphite and are labeled with the letter B. Of the pencils listed, 6B would represent the softest graphite. The correct answer, therefore, is (B).

45. Used for cleaning or thinning watercolor, gouache, acrylic, and water-miscible oils, water is the most common solvent used in studio processes. The correct answer, therefore, is (D).

46. In the context of drawing, "modeling" means varying value to create the illusion of three-dimensional form. Although the other choices relate to creating the illusion of form or space, none of them does so by manipulating value. The correct answer, therefore, is (C).

47. The vehicle is the "carrier" liquid in which pigment is suspended to form paint. The correct answer, therefore, is (B).

48. There are two basic steps in creating a papier-mâché object. First an armature, or wire frame, is made. Next, a paste is smeared liberally on the form and torn or cut strips of newsprint are applied to the wet paste. This process continues until several layers have been built up for strength and the form developed. The correct answer, therefore, is (A).

49. Less tacky than the other answer choices listed and unlikely to damage the surface of the paper when removed, masking tape is most commonly used to mask the portions of a picture to be kept free of paint, charcoal, and other materials in hard-edge painting. The correct answer, therefore, is (C).

50. Of the pottery terms listed, "coil" and "slab" are techniques for hand-building clay. The correct answer, therefore, is (A).

51. Thickly applied opaque paint, often deliberately standing up from the surface and showing the brushstrokes or other instrument of application, describes a technique known as impasto. The correct answer, therefore, is (A).

52. A gray made from a mixture of complementary colors is chromatic. The correct answer, therefore, is (B).

53. The adjustable lens opening, indicated in f/stop numbers, that determines the amount of light allowed to pass through the lens is the aperture. The correct answer, therefore, is (D).

54. The nib and penholder are components of a technical pen; the quill, of a dip pen. A stump is a cylinder of compressed paper or felt used to blend pastel, charcoal, and pencil. The correct answer, therefore, is (B).

55. To obtain a bird's-eye or worm's-eye view of an object, one would utilize the vanishing points on the horizon (or eye level) and add a third point either above or below the horizon. This linear perspective is three-point. The correct answer, therefore, is (D).

56. The burin and the squeegee are both used during the printmaking process. The burin is a narrow, v-shaped gouge used to create the lines in an engraving; a squeegee is a rubber blade used to force ink through the screen in serigraphy. The correct answer, therefore, is (A).

57. The degree of detail in a digital image, particularly its sharpness, is stated in terms of high or low resolution. The correct answer, therefore, is (B).

58. The decoration achieved by soldering fine metal wires to a metal background, creating small cells or cloisons, is cloisonné. These cells are then filled with moistened enamel powders and fired to create a hard decorative surface. The correct answer, therefore, is (C).

59. To obtain its optimum density, true porcelain is fired at temperatures above 2,300 F, which is the highest firing temperature required by any of the clays listed. The correct answer, therefore, is (D).

60. Computer printers use chromatic mode, in which the colors are defined by the elements cyan, magenta, yellow, and black, or CMYK. The correct answer, therefore, is (D).

61. In painting, "scumbling" refers to a layer of opaque or semiopaque paint that is lightly applied over a previously dried layer so the lower layer of paint is not completely obliterated and shows through irregularly. Scumbling gives an uneven, broken effect to the brushed-on color. The correct answer, therefore, is (C).

62. Turpentine has a very low PEL (permissible exposure level), and, in addition to emitting harmful vapors, it can be absorbed through healthy, unbroken skin. The correct answer, therefore, is (A).

63. Serigraphy is also known as silk-screen printing and comes from the Latin *sericum*, or "silk." The essence of the technique is that a fine mesh screen, stretched tightly over a wooden frame, is placed above a sheet of paper and ink or paint is forced through the mesh with a rubber blade called a squeegee. The correct answer, therefore, is (A).

64. The lost-wax process has been used for centuries to cast molten metal into hollow plaster molds lined with wax. The wax becomes "lost" when it melts later in the process as the mold is heated. The correct answer, therefore, is (C).

65. The acids found in an etching bath produce fumes that can cause physical disorders if used in a poorly ventilated room. The correct answer, therefore, is (D).

66. All of the choices refer to digital imagery, but only "bitmap" refers to arrangements of dots that store information. The correct response, therefore, is (D).

67. To temporarily protect part of a water-based painting from absorbing paint or ink, an easily removable mask or frisket is used. There are two basic types of frisket: a liquid that is painted on or a solid that can be cut to fit the area to be protected. The correct answer, therefore, is (A).

68. Painting or drawing with small dots of paint, ink, graphite, etc., is called stippling. Graduated tones of lightness and darkness can be achieved by varying the size of the dots, or more commonly by adjusting the proximity of the dots to one another. The particular form of stippling used in this piece by Seurat is called pointillism. The correct answer, therefore, is (B).

69. Of the printmaking processes listed, lithography, stenciling, and intaglio require an image to be drawn, etched, or stenciled onto a flat surface onto which ink is then forced. Collagraphy is an additive process by which a print is both inked and textured. A three-dimensional surface is built up using a variety of materials, ink is applied, and the plate is run through an etching press. The paper is forced into the inked depressions, and the result is both inking and some embossing. The correct answer, therefore, is (B).

70. A roller made of hard rubber and used to apply ink to a printing surface is a brayer. The correct answer, therefore, is (D).

Chapter 7
Succeeding on the Art Constructed-Response Tests

▶ ▶ ▶ ▶ ▶ ▶ ▶ ▶ ▶ ▶ ▶ ▶ ▶

This chapter provides advice for maximizing your success on the Art constructed-response tests, with special focus on the scoring guides and procedures used by the scorers. Chapters 8 and 11 offer step-by-step strategies for working through questions, lists of the topics covered, and lists of sources you can use to prepare.

TIP Advice from the Experts

Scorers who have scored hundreds of actual tests were asked to give advice to teacher candidates planning to take the Art constructed-response tests. The scorers' advice boiled down to the practical suggestions given below.

1. **Read and answer the question accurately.** Be sure to dissect the parts of the question and analyze what each part is asking you to do. If the question asks you to describe or discuss, keep that requirement in mind when composing your response—do not just give a list.

2. **Answer everything that is asked in the question.** Many test takers fail to provide a complete response. If a question asks you to do three distinct things in your response, don't give a response to just two of those things. No matter how well you write about those two things, the scorers will not award you full credit.

3. **Give a thorough and detailed response.** Your response must indicate to the scorers that you have a thorough understanding of the applicable principles and guidelines related to teaching art. The scorers will not read into your response any information that is not specifically stated. If something is not written, they do not know that you know it and will not give you credit for it.

   A word of caution: Superfluous writing will obscure your points and will make it difficult for the scorers to be confident of your full understanding of the material. Be straightforward in your response. Do not try to impress the scorers. If you do not know the answer, you cannot receive full credit, but if you do know the answer, provide enough information to convince the scorers that you have a full understanding of the topic.

4. **Do not change the question or challenge the basis of the question.** Stay focused on the question that is asked. You will receive no credit or, at best, a low score if you choose to answer another question or if you state, for example, that there is no possible answer. Answer the question by addressing the fundamental issues. Do not venture off topic to demonstrate your particular field of expertise if it is not specifically related to the question. This undermines the impression that you understand the concept adequately.

5. **Reread your response, both to improve your writing (for the essays test) and to check that you have written what you thought you wrote.** Frequently, sentences are left unfinished or clarifying information is omitted.

General Scoring Guides for the Art Constructed-Response Tests

The scorers' advice above corresponds with the official scoring criteria used at scoring sessions. It is a good idea to be familiar with the scoring rubrics so you can maximize your success and spend your time on things that matter (e.g., demonstrating understanding of the selection and providing good examples) rather than spending time on things that don't matter (e.g., writing a very long essay, making copious citations).

General Scoring Guide for the *Art Making* Test

The following scoring guide provides the overarching framework for scoring the essay questions in the *Art Making* test.

As discussed in chapter 1, there are two 5-minute questions and two 25-minute questions on the *Art Making* test. The 5-minute questions are scored on a scale from 0 to 3. The 25-minute questions are scored on a scale of 0 to 5. Following is the general scoring guide used to score the 5-minute questions:

General Scoring Guide for the 5-Minute Exercises

Score	Comment
3	■ Shows full understanding of the issues and concepts presented by the question ■ Provides sufficient, appropriate, and accurate details or examples to support and amplify general statements ■ Discusses all parts of the question appropriately; response shows superior organization, clarity, focus, and cohesiveness ■ Makes insightful observations about textual and/or visual materials presented in the question; thoroughly analyzes relational issues when these are implied in the question ■ Uses an extensive art vocabulary that is accurate and appropriate
2	■ Shows basic understanding of the issues and concepts presented by the question ■ Provides appropriate details or examples to support and amplify general statements ■ Discusses the major parts of the question adequately; response shows acceptable organization, clarity, focus, and cohesiveness ■ Makes accurate observations about textual and/or visual materials presented in the question; clearly analyzes relational issues when these are implied in the question ■ Uses an adequate art vocabulary that is accurate and appropriate
1	■ Shows little or no understanding of the issues and concepts presented by the question ■ Provides inappropriate details or no details or examples to support and amplify general statements ■ Ignores major parts of the question; response is unfocused, lacks cohesion, and exhibits serious flaws in communication skills ■ Makes illogical or inappropriate observations about textual and/or visual materials presented in the question; misses many relational issues when these are implied in the question ■ Uses incorrect or no art terminology
0	■ Blank or off-topic response

Following is the general scoring guide used to score the 25-minute questions:

General Scoring Guide for the 25-Minute Essay Questions

Score	Comment

5
- Shows full understanding of the issues and concepts presented by the question
- Provides a sufficient number of appropriate and accurate details or examples to support and amplify general statements
- Discusses all parts of the question thoroughly; response shows superior organization, clarity, focus, and cohesiveness
- Makes in-depth, insightful observations about his or her work; thoroughly analyzes relational issues when these are implied in the question
- Uses an extensive art vocabulary that is accurate and appropriate

4
- Shows substantial understanding of the issues and concepts presented by the question
- Provides appropriate and accurate details or examples to support and amplify general statements
- Discusses the major parts of the question thoroughly; response shows good organization, clarity, focus, and cohesiveness
- Makes in-depth observations about his or her work; clearly analyzes relational issues when these are implied in the question
- Uses art vocabulary appropriately and accurately.

3
- Shows basic understanding of the significant issues and concepts presented by the question
- Provides basically correct and appropriate details or examples to support and amplify general statements
- Discusses the major parts of the question adequately; response shows acceptable organization, clarity, focus, and cohesiveness
- Makes accurate or appropriate observations about his or her work; adequately analyzes relational issues when these are implied in the question
- In most cases, uses art vocabulary appropriately and accurately

Score		Comment

2
- Shows limited understanding of the issues and concepts presented by the question
- Provides some inappropriate details or no details or examples to support and amplify general statements
- Discusses the major parts of the question inadequately or in a limited manner; response shows weak organization, lacks clarity, focus, and cohesiveness, and exhibits flaws in communication skills
- Makes some illogical or inappropriate observations about his or her work; misses many relational issues when these are implied in the question
- Uses some art terms inaccurately

1
- Shows little or no understanding of the issues and concepts presented by the question
- Provides inappropriate details or no details or examples to support and amplify general statements
- Ignores major parts of the question; response is unfocused, lacks cohesion, and exhibits serious flaws in communication skills
- Makes illogical or inappropriate observations about his or her work; misses many relational issues when these are implied in the question
- Uses incorrect or no art terminology

0
- Blank or off-topic response

General Scoring Guide for the *Art: Content, Traditions, Aesthetics, and Criticisms* Test

The following scoring guide provides the overarching framework for scoring the questions in the *Art: Content, Traditions, Aesthetics, and Criticisms* test.

As discussed in chapter 1, there are three 20-minute questions on the *Art: CTAC* test. The questions are scored on a scale of 0 to 5.

General Scoring Guide for the 20-Minute Essay Questions

Score	Comment

5
- Shows full understanding of the issues and concepts presented by the question
- Provides a sufficient number of appropriate and accurate details or examples to support and amplify general statements
- Discusses all parts of the question thoroughly; response is clear and focused throughout
- Makes in-depth, insightful observations about textual and/or visual materials presented in the question; thoroughly analyzes relational issues when these are implied in the question
- Uses an extensive art vocabulary that is accurate and appropriate

4
- Shows substantial understanding of the issues and concepts presented by the question
- Provides appropriate and accurate details or examples to support and amplify general statements
- Discusses the major parts of the question thoroughly; response is generally clear and focused
- Makes in-depth observations about textual and/or visual materials presented in the question; clearly analyzes relational issues when these are implied in the question
- Uses art vocabulary appropriately and accurately

3
- Shows basic understanding of the significant issues and concepts presented by the question
- Provides basically correct and appropriate details or examples to support and amplify general statements
- Discusses the major parts of the question adequately; response is inconsistent with respect to clarity and/or focus
- Makes accurate or appropriate observations about textual and/or visual materials presented in the question; adequately analyzes relational issues when these are implied in the question
- In most cases, uses art vocabulary appropriately and accurately

Score		Comment

2
- Shows limited understanding of the issues and concepts presented by the question
- Provides some inappropriate details or no details or examples to support and amplify general statements
- Discusses the major parts of the question inadequately or in a limited manner; most of the response lacks clarity and/or focus
- Makes some illogical or inappropriate observations about textual and/or visual materials presented in the question; misses many relational issues when these are implied in the question
- Uses some art terms accurately

1
- Shows little or no understanding of the issues and concepts presented by the question
- Provides inappropriate details or no details or examples to support and amplify general statements
- Ignores major parts of the question; response is consistently unfocused and/or unclear
- Makes illogical or inappropriate observations about textual and/or visual materials presented in the question; misses many relational issues when these are implied in the question
- Uses incorrect or no art terminology

0
- Blank or off-topic response

What You Should Know About How the Art Constructed-Response Tests Are Scored

As you build your skills in writing answers to constructed-response questions, it is important to have in mind the process used to score the tests. If you understand the process by which experts determine your scores, you may have a better context in which to think about your strategies for success.

How the Tests Are Scored

After each test administration, test books are returned to ETS. The test books in which constructed-response answers are written are sent to the location of the scoring session.

The scoring sessions usually take place over two days. The sessions are led by scoring leaders, highly qualified art teachers who have many years of experience scoring test questions. All the remaining scorers are experienced art teachers and art teacher educators. An effort is made to balance experienced scorers with newer scorers at each session; the experienced scorers provide continuity with past sessions, and the new scorers ensure that new ideas and perspectives are considered and that the pool of scorers remains large enough to cover the test's needs throughout the year.

Preparing to Train the Scorers

The scoring leaders meet several days before the scoring session to assemble the materials for the training portions of the main session. Training scorers is a rigorous process, and it is designed to ensure that each response gets a score that is consistent with both the scores given to other papers and the overall scoring philosophy and criteria established for the test when it was designed.

The scoring leaders first review the "General Scoring Guides," which contain the overall criteria, stated in general terms, for awarding the appropriate score. The leaders also review and discuss—and make additions to, if necessary—the "Question-Specific Scoring Guides," which serve as applications of the general guide to each specific question on the test. The question-specific guides cannot cover every possible response the scorers will see, but they are designed to give enough examples to guide the scorers in making accurate judgments about the variety of answers they will encounter.

To begin identifying appropriate training materials for an individual question, the scoring leaders first read through many responses to get a sense of the range of answers. They then choose a set of benchmarks, one paper at each score level. These benchmarks serve as solid representative examples of the kind of response that meets the scoring criteria at each score level and are considered the foundation for score standards throughout the session.

The scoring leaders then choose a larger set of test taker responses to serve as sample papers that represent the wide variety of possible responses the scorers might see. The sample papers serve as the basis for practice scoring at the scoring session, so the scorers can rehearse how they will apply the scoring criteria before they begin.

The process of choosing a set of benchmark responses and a set of sample responses is followed systematically for each question to be scored at the session. After the scoring leaders have completed their selections and discussions, the sets they have chosen are photocopied and inserted into the scorers' folders in preparation for the session.

Training at the Main Scoring Session

At the scoring session, the scorers are placed into groups according to the question they are assigned to score. New scorers are distributed equally across all groups. One of the scoring leaders is placed with each group. The "chief scorer" is the person who has overall authority over the scoring session and plays a variety of key roles in training and in ensuring consistent and fair scores.

For each question, the training session proceeds in the same way:

1. All scorers carefully read through the question they will be scoring.

2. All scorers review the "General Scoring Guide" and the "Question-Specific Scoring Guide" for the question.

3. For each question, the leader guides the scorers through the set of benchmark responses, explaining in detail why each response received the score it did. Scorers are encouraged to ask questions and share their perspectives.

4. Scorers then practice on the set of sample responses chosen by the leader. The leader polls the scorers on what scores they would award and then leads a discussion to ensure there is a consensus about the scoring criteria and how they are to be applied.

5. When the leader is confident that the scorers for that question will apply the criteria consistently and accurately, the actual scoring begins.

Quality-Control Processes

A number of procedures are followed to ensure that accuracy of scoring is maintained during the scoring session. Most importantly, each response is scored twice, with the first scorer's decision hidden from the second scorer. If the two scores for a paper are the same or differ by only one point, the scoring for that paper is considered complete, and the test taker will be awarded the sum of the two scores. If the two scores differ by more than one point, the response is scored by a scoring leader, who has not seen the decisions made by the other two scorers. If this third score is midway between the first two scores, the test taker's score for the question is the sum of the first two scores; otherwise, it is the sum of the third score and whichever of the first two scores is closer to it.

Another way of maintaining scoring accuracy is through back-reading. Throughout the session, the leader for each question checks random samples of scores awarded by all the scorers. If the leader finds that a scorer is not applying the scoring criteria appropriately, that scorer is given more training.

At the beginning of the second day of reading, additional sets of papers are scored using the consensus method described above. This helps ensure that the scorers are refreshed on the scoring criteria and are applying them consistently.

Finally, the scoring session is designed so that several different scorers contribute to any single test taker's total score. This minimizes the effects of a scorer who might score slightly more stringently or generously than other scorers.

The entire scoring process—general and specific scoring guides, standardized benchmarks and samples, consensus scoring, adjudication procedures, back-reading, and rotation of test questions to a variety of scorers—is applied consistently and systematically at every scoring session to ensure comparable scores for each administration and across all administrations of the test.

Given the information above about how constructed responses are scored and what the scorers are looking for in successful responses, you are now ready to look at specific questions, suggestions of how to approach the questions, and sample responses and scores given to those responses.

Chapter 8
Preparing for the *Art Making* Test

► ► ► ► ► ► ► ► ► ► ► ►

The goal of this chapter is to provide you with strategies for how to read, analyze, and understand the questions on the *Art Making* test and then how to outline and write successful responses to the questions.

Introduction to the Test

The *Art Making* test is intended primarily for people who are completing teacher-education programs and who plan to become teachers of art. Test takers have typically completed a bachelor's degree program in art or art education.

The test is composed of **two 5-minute exercises and two 25-minute essays**.

The five-minute exercises are designed to measure working knowledge and skills associated with elements and principles of design and their application, as well as basic art media and processes. The exercises require the test taker to demonstrate a working knowledge of the skills and techniques associated with the following media or processes:

- drawing, including pencil, charcoal, pen and brush, pen and ink, chalk, pastels, and conte
- painting, including oil, watercolor, and acrylic
- printmaking, including intaglio, lithography, silk screen, relief printing, and monoprints
- sculpture, including wood, fiber, clay, plastic, and plaster
- ceramics, including clay, glazes, and other decorations
- crafts
- technology/media, including computer graphics, video, and photography

The demonstration may take the form of describing the general steps, stages, or techniques associated with the media or processes, or it may require the test taker to apply knowledge of basic art concepts (such as elements and principles of design), skills, or techniques. In some cases, the exercise may require actual demonstration of basic skills that can be executed in the test book with a pencil or pen.

The two 25-minute responses ask the test taker to demonstrate the ability to discuss work that he or she has created. The responses document personal art making and require the test taker to bring four color photographs or still reproductions of his or her own artwork.

- Each image must be of a different work.
- Each of the images must be clear and show the complete artwork.
- At least two of the artworks represented must be in a medium or media that are not used in any of the other artworks.

Because the two responses MUST be written about work in two different media, the photos or other reproductions should not all show work in the same medium. If the two responses refer to work in the same medium, or media that are virtually indistinguishable from each other, the second response **will not** be scored. Note that the responses are scored on the basis of how well the test taker is able to write about his or her work; a response can be successful even if it is based on a work that the test taker does not consider to be his or her best work.

Some examples of media that are NOT sufficiently different for the two responses would include (but are not limited to) the following:

- an acrylic painting and a painting that combines acrylics with a second medium
- a photograph and a digitally altered version of a photograph
- a digitally altered version of a photograph and a computer-generated graphic
- two plaster sculptures, one cast and the other carved
- a watercolor painting and a wash painting using another kind of paint
- a pen-and-ink drawing and a pen-and-ink drawing with a watercolor wash
- a wheel-thrown clay pot and a coil pot

Many examples of media that are sufficiently different are, of course, obvious (e.g., a painting and a sculpture; a drawing and a piece of jewelry; a photograph and a drawing). There are endless possibilities. Closer examples that are acceptable would include (but are not limited to) the following:

- an impasto oil painting and a watercolor
- a cast plaster sculpture and a welded metal sculpture
- a pastel drawing and an unrelated print
- a clay-slab vessel and a similar vessel constructed of wood or found objects
- a photograph and a collage of various kinds of paper, including pieces from magazine pages

The questions ask the test taker to write about his or her work in relation to the following topics:

- which process you used to make the work and why you selected it
- what artistic concepts underlie the work
- how you selected the theme of the work and how that theme was expressed
- the knowledge you gained as part of the process of creating the work
- how the work was generated from inception to final work
- the art-related and other influences on the art-making process
- how you evaluate or critique your work
- the tools, materials, and techniques you used in making the work
- what place the work holds in your personal artistic development
- the art elements and principles of composition that you incorporated into your work

What to Study

Success on this test is not simply a matter of learning more about how to respond to different types of constructed-response questions. It also takes real knowledge of the field. As mentioned above, the test is designed to gather evidence about your knowledge of and skills associated with elements and principles of design and their application, as well as basic art media and processes and your ability to discuss work that you have created.

It therefore would serve you well to read books and review notes in the area of art making.

The following books, periodicals, and Web sites are particularly relevant to the content covered by the test. **Note:** The test is not based on these resources, and they do not necessarily cover every topic that may be included in the test.

Books

Atkins, Robert. *ArtSpeak: A Guide to Contemporary Ideas, Movements and Buzzwords*, Abbeville Press, 1990.
   A book of essays and timeline of Post WWII art and art criticism.

Bruber, Felton. *A Sculptor's Guide to Tools and Materials*, A.B.F.S Publishing, 2000.
   A resource for sculptors in various media that includes a guide for selecting tools and materials.

Clarke, Michael. *The Concise Oxford Dictionary of Art Terms*, Oxford University Press, 2001.
   Written by the Director of the National Gallery of Scotland; more than 1,800 entries cover periods, styles, materials, techniques, and foreign terms.

Enstice, Wayne, and Melody Peters. *Drawing Space, Form, and Expression*, 3rd ed. Prentice Hall, 2003.
   This book covers a wealth of drawing information, including perspective, various uses of form, color, the human figure, and visualization.

Gilbert, Rita. *Living with Art*, 5th ed. McGraw-Hill, 1998.
   Art appreciation text with a comprehensive discussion of the themes, purposes, and elements of art.

Itten, Johannes. *The Elements of Color*, Wiley, 1997.
   This book presents theories on color and includes practical exercises.

Lauer, David. *Design Basics*, 6th ed., Wadsworth, 2004.
   This book illustrates what design is/should be through visual examples from different time periods and various cultures.

Mayer, Ralph. *The Artists' Handbook of Materials and Techniques*, 5th ed. Viking, 1991.
   This book has a wealth of information, charts, and line drawings, and is a reference for painters, sculptors and printmakers.

Ocvirk, Otto G., et al. *Art Fundamentals*, 9th ed., McGraw Hill, 2002.
   This book goes over the basic compositional issues in depth, then moves on to content and style.

Poore, Henry. *Composition in Art*, Dover, 1991.
This book demonstrates the principles of composition through analysis of works from the Middle Ages to the present.

Robertson, Jean, and Craig McDaniel. *Painting as Language*, Wadsworth, 1999.
This book covers all aspects of painting, from getting started, materials, techniques, and color, to narrative painting, abstraction, and social issues.

Stephenson, Jonathan. *The Materials and Techniques of Painting*, Thames & Hudson, 1993.
A comprehensive guide to the materials and techniques of painting.

Sturken, Marita. *Practices of Looking: An Introduction to Visual Culture*, Oxford University Press, 2001.
This book explores the visual analysis of painting, photography, and new media.

Taylor, Joshua. *Learning to Look: A Handbook for the Visual Arts*, University of Chicago Press, 1981.

Zelanski, Paul, and Mary Pat Fisher. *Shaping Space*, Wadsworth, 1994.
This is a concise book that deals with all aspects of developing a two-dimensional space.

Zelanski, Paul, and Mary Pat Fisher. *The Art of Seeing*, Pearson Education, 2004.
A good reference book with a discussion of history, compositional issues, and so on.

Zelanski, Paul, and Mary Pat Fisher. *Design Principles and Problems*, Wadsworth, 1995.
This book covers principles of addressing both two- and three-dimensional space, and includes terminology for both areas.

Periodicals

Art News, published monthly, includes artist profiles, museum-exhibition news and reviews, and news and inside reports on events and issues that shape the art world.
48 West 38th Street, New York, NY 10018

Art in America, published monthly, creates a fascinating picture of the art world—the colorful and often controversial art scene here and abroad.
575 Broadway, Fifth Floor, New York, NY 10012

ArtForum, published 10 times per year, includes features, news, reviews, and editorials.
350 Seventh Ave, New York, NY 10001

Art Times, published monthly, includes editorials, reviews, artist profiles, and art criticism.
PO Box 730, Mt. Marion, NY 12456-0730

American Artist, published monthly, includes technical information and articles on the visual arts.
BPI Communications, 1515 Broadway, New York, NY 10036

The Artist's Magazine, published monthly, includes technical information and articles on the visual arts.
F&W Publications, 1507 Dana Avenue, Cincinnati, OH 45207

Web Sites

www.artlex.com
ArtLex is an online dictionary of visual art that focuses on aesthetics along with art production, art history, art criticism, and art education.

www.aesthetics-online.org
This is the official Web site of the American Society for Aesthetics.

Understanding What the Questions Are Asking

The first important factor in creating a successful response to a question is to understand the question thoroughly. Often, test takers jump into their responses without taking enough time to analyze exactly what the question is asking or how many different parts of the question need to be addressed. The time you invest in making sure you understand what the question is asking will very likely pay off in a better performance. Ideally, you want to use enough of your time reading to make sure you do understand the question, but not so much that you are left with an insufficient amount of time for writing.

Examine the overall question closely, then identify what specific questions are being asked, mentally organize your response, and outline your ideas. Leave yourself plenty of time to write (or draw, if appropriate) your answer. If you think out your response beforehand, your response will probably be stronger.

To illustrate the importance of understanding the question before you begin writing, let's start with a sample question.

Five-Minute Exercise

The following exercise, intended to take approximately five minutes to answer, is designed to assess the test taker's knowledge of basic art-making procedures.

Sample Question 1

Choose three of the four basic forms (cylinder, sphere, cone, cube) and draw a composition in which the forms are arranged so that at least two of them overlap. In your composition you should

- draw a horizon line

- indicate the direction of a main source of light

- shade the forms to give the illusion of three dimensions

- include cast shadows

- outline the limits of the composition

Identifying the Key Components of the Question

There are *five requirements* in the question:

Draw a composition of three objects from the list of forms provided. In drawing your composition, you are asked to meet the following specific criteria:

- Include three objects, at least two overlapping.

- Create a horizon line.

- Label the light source.

- Use shading and cast shadows to define the forms and the source of light.

- Draw a line to set the limits of the composition.

Organizing Your Response

Successful responses start with understanding and successful planning. The point of this exercise is to see whether you understand how to create simple forms that convey the illusion of solidity through shading and how to shade the forms and create shadows that appear to come from a consistent light source. You don't have to make a polished drawing to do well on the question; what you need to do is produce a drawing that demonstrates your understanding. It is important to plan, because all parts of the question must be present for you to receive a good score; by planning your response, you greatly decrease the chances that you will forget to incorporate any part of the exercise. Your note-taking space gives you a place to jot down a quick sketch and key words, if those are helpful. In the case of the five-minute exercises, you must keep track of the time so you leave sufficient time to draw your response within this brief framework.

To illustrate a possible strategy for planning a response, focus again on the sample exercise introduced above. We analyzed the exercise and found that it asked for a drawn response. You might begin by drawing the forms you have chosen from the four listed on your notes page and writing the following: *horizon, light source, shading and cast shadow, outline*. This will ensure that you address each part when you begin drawing.

Main Parts to Be Addressed

I. Three forms

II. Horizon

III. Light source

IV. Shading and cast shadow

V. Outline

Organizing the Composition

You then might organize the composition in your mind and think of how to place the objects on the test area. Fill out the components of the exercise that need to be addressed:

I. **Three shapes**
Draw shapes to overlap.

II. **Horizon**
Create a context—a place in which to place the forms.

III. **Light source**
Label the light source.

IV. **Shading and cast shadow**
Use shading of the forms to create the illusion of three dimensions; use the shading and cast shadows to indicate where the light source is.

V. **Outline**
Use the outline to define the limits of the composition.

Drawing Your Response

Now the important step of drawing your response begins. The scorers will not consider your notes when they score your paper, so it is crucial that you integrate all the important ideas from your notes into your actual drawn response.

Some test takers believe that every drawn response on a Praxis test has to be a masterpiece—that is, a skillfully drawn, fully finished work of art. The *Art Making* test does **not** require your drawing to be a personal best, so you should use techniques that allow you to communicate information efficiently and clearly. For example, you might choose to use hatching to show shading if that is something you can execute quickly.

Returning to our sample exercise, see below how the outline of the response to the first part of the question can become the final drawn response. What follows is an actual response by a test taker.

Sample Response That Received a Score of 2

You can see in the following annotated version how the sample response incorporates each of the points that were outlined above.

Sample Response with Annotations

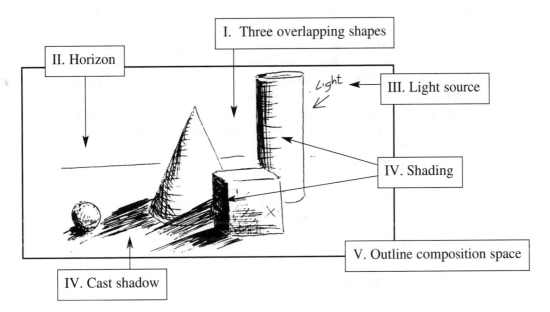

Twenty-Five-Minute Essay

The following question is a sample of a 25-minute essay question that is to be answered with reference to one of the reproductions of your work.

Use one of the artworks you have brought to answer the following question.

Part A: How did your knowledge and experience of other artists' works, other styles, or other periods affect your choice of medium and/or style and/or technique?

Part B: Describe the expressive or thematic idea(s) you explored in this work. How do these ideas interact with the medium and/or style and/or technique of the work?

Part C: Why is this work significant to you? What does this work say about your personal artistic development or your response to social issues?

Identifying the Key Components of the Question

There are three parts to the question. However, each of the three offers you choices, so you can respond to the question in the way that is most appropriate for you and your work. For your response to Part A and Part B, you might discuss only one of the possibilities listed—medium, style, or technique. Or you might decide to respond by discussing any two or all three. Your essay would not be scored on the basis of how many of those aspects you discussed, but on how well you wrote about whichever you chose to focus on. Part C provides a similar choice. If your work has a strong connection to social issues, you could write about that; on the other hand, if that aspect of art is not part of what you were doing, you could focus your response on your own development as an artist. Here, too, a combination of both ideas would be fine.

There are actually *four parts* to the question:

- Choose the work you will write about.

- Discuss the interaction between an outside source and your own work's medium, style, and/or technique.

- Discuss the interaction of the expressive or thematic aspects of your work with its medium, style, and/or technique.

- Discuss the significance of the work in terms of your development or social concerns.

Organizing Your Response

Successful responses start with successful planning, either with an outline or with another form of notes. By planning your response, you greatly decrease the chances that you will forget to answer any part of the question. You increase the chances of creating a well-organized response, which is something the scorers look for. Your note-taking space also gives you a place to jot down thoughts whenever you think of them—for example, when you have an idea about one part of the question while you are writing your response to another part. Like taking time to make sure you understand what the question is asking, planning your response is time well invested, although you must keep track of the time so that you leave enough to write your response.

To illustrate a possible strategy for planning a response, focus again on the sample question introduced in the previous section. Because it is not possible to discuss this kind of essay without looking at the art that is being discussed, we will analyze this question based on a sample response. The artwork for the response appears on page 178 of appendix C. Pretend that you are writing about this work. You might begin by jotting down those parts on your notes page, leaving space under each. This will ensure that you address each part when you begin writing.

Sample Notes—Main Parts to be Answered

Here you start by identifying each part of the question:

I. Choose work

II. Outside source + my work's medium, style, technique

III. My work's expressiveness or idea + medium, style, technique

IV. My development or social concerns in work

You then might quickly fill out the main ideas you want to address in each part, like this:

Sample Notes—Ideas Under Each Main Part

I. Choose work
   —Photo

II. Outside source + my work's medium, style, technique
   —Photo history

III. My work's expressiveness or idea + medium, style, technique
   —Deconstruction
   —Series

IV. My development or social concerns in work
   —Success of ideas
   —Not socially related

To earn the highest number of points from the scorers, you will need to do all of the following:

- Answer all parts of the question.
- Give reasons for your answers.
- Demonstrate knowledge of art making in your answer.

Now look at your notes and add any ideas that would address these characteristics. Notice below the additions that are made.

Sample Notes—With Added Ideas

This is where you use your knowledge of art making together with your own thinking about art and what you value in your work. Remember that these essays are not scored on the basis of value judgments about the art you have made; the scoring is based on how clearly and thoughtfully you are able to respond in the context of discussing your own work. For the sample essay, the expanded notes look like this:

I. Choose work
—Photo
   Use photo of lighthouse lawn ornament—fits with idea of other artists' work

II. Outside source + my work's medium, style, technique
—Photo history, art theory
   Lartigue
   Reaction to postmodern idea of deconstruction—good/bad, beautiful/ugly
   Does not have to be dramatic or political; can be lighthearted, still aesthetically
      interesting

III. My work's expressiveness or idea + medium, style, technique
—Deconstruction
   Taking something piece by piece out of context
—Series
   Part of series with cut-outs and dodging, where systematically recognizable
      context was removed

IV. My development or social concerns in work
—Success of idea
   Significant because of its success in becoming unrecognizable
—Not socially related
   Commentary that art can be, but is not required to be, politically/socially related

You have now created the skeleton of your written response.

Writing Your Response

Now the important step of writing your response begins. The scorers will not consider your notes when they score your paper, so it is crucial that you integrate all the important ideas from your notes into your actual written response.

Some test takers believe that every written response on a Praxis test has to be in formal essay form—that is, with an introductory paragraph, then paragraphs with the response to the question, then a concluding paragraph. This is the case for very few Praxis tests (e.g., *Writing*). The *Art Making* test does **not** require formal essays, so you should use techniques that allow you to communicate information efficiently and clearly. For example, you can use bulleted or numbered lists, or a chart, or a combination of essay and chart. Whatever format you choose, the response should be as clear as possible, and you should be careful to support your ideas with specific references to the artwork you are discussing.

Returning to the sample question, see below how the outline of the response to the first part of the question can become the final written response. What follows is an actual response by a test taker.

Sample Response

Refer to page 178 of appendix C for an image of the artwork for this sample response.

Part A

Jaque Henri Lartigue did not set out to become an artist. He was a boy with the means to explore a new development in image creation. To him photography was the perfect method of capturing scenes he wished to remember. The series to which this photograph belongs is deeply influenced by Lartigue's pure love of taking photos and his focus on enjoyable images even in troubled times. Building off that basis, the photograph is also a reaction to the postmodern idea of deconstruction. To break something down, find nuances, does not automatically determine that the subject must have the duality of showing both the beautiful and ugly. Art does not have to be dramatic or political, it can be light hearted and still aesthetically interesting.

Part B

With this image, I chose to interpret deconstruction as taking out of context. The original subject is a small lighthouse lawn ornament sitting in front of a cinderblock wall. In the spirit of Lartigue, it is something I encountered which I found humorous. The photo is the second in a series of 6. Using paper cutouts during development, I was able to remove the background of the photo leaving just the lighthouse. Through the series I systematically removed or added elements to change the context of the subject, or even remove the subject from the context, always maintaining the initial feeling of humor. The manipulation of context is enhanced through the use of photography over other media.

Part C

This particular image is significant due to its success in becoming unrecognizable as a photo of a lawn ornament. Even while sitting in a rinse tray in the darkroom, people were puzzled over whether or not it actually was a photo, and not some sort of drawing reproduction. The image also is a commentary on my belief that art is not required to be politically or socially motivated.

In Conclusion

Whatever format you select, the important thing is that your answer be thorough, complete, and detailed.

For the drawing responses, be certain to do the following:

- Answer all parts of the question.
- Produce a drawing that demonstrates your understanding of the art-making concept being tested.

For the essay responses, be certain to do the following:

- Answer all parts of the question.
- Give reasons for your answers.
- Demonstrate knowledge of art making in your answer.

It is a good idea to use the practice test in the next chapter to help develop a plan for how you will take the test on the actual testing day, especially if you tend to get nervous or "freeze up" in a testing situation. Whatever format you select for your essay, the important thing is that your answer be thorough, complete, and detailed.

Chapter 9
Practice Questions—*Art Making*

► ► ► ► ► ► ► ► ► ► ► ►

Now that you have studied the content topics and have worked through strategies relating to constructed-response questions, you should answer the following practice questions. You will probably find it helpful to simulate actual testing conditions, giving yourself 60 minutes to work on the questions. You can cut out and use the response pages provided if you wish.

Keep in mind that the test you take at an actual administration will have different questions, although the number of questions of each type will be the same. You should not expect your responses to these practice questions to be at exactly the same level as when you take the test at an actual administration, because numerous factors affect a person's performance in any given testing situation.

When you have finished the practice questions, you can look at sample responses and read the explanations for the scores they received in chapter 10.

Professional Assessments for Beginning Teachers ®

TEST NAME:

Art Making

4 Practice Questions

Time—60 Minutes

SECTION A: BASIC PROCEDURES

Questions 1–2
(Suggested time—10 minutes)

Directions: This section of the test contains two questions. You are expected to answer both. Allow yourself approximately five minutes to answer each question.

Write your answers to the following questions on the pages indicated. Your answers may take the form of a brief paragraph, a list, an outline, or a labeled sketch or diagram.

Question 1
(Suggested time—5 minutes)

Part A

Briefly define the following terms.

- Form
- Contrast
- Negative space

Part B

Briefly explain how painters or sculptors might use form, contrast, and negative space in their work.

Begin your response on page 76.

(Question 1—*Continued*)

Respond to **Question 1** in the space provided below.

Part A

Briefly define the following terms.

Form:

Contrast:

Negative space:

Part B

Briefly explain how painters or sculptors might use form, contrast, and negative space in their work.

Question 2
(Suggested time—5 minutes)

In the three labeled spaces provided on page 78, draw an exterior view of a cube that demonstrates the type of perspective indicated in each space.

■ The minimum length for any side of the cubes you draw should be about 1 to 1½ inches.

Begin your response on page 78.

(Question 2—*Continued*)

Respond to **Question 2** in the spaces provided below.

One-point perspective

Two-point perspective

Three-point perspective

SECTION B: BASIC PROCEDURES

Questions 3–4
(Suggested time—50 minutes)

Directions: This section of the test contains two questions. You are expected to answer both. Allow yourself approximately 25 minutes to answer each question. For each question, you are to discuss <u>ONLY ONE</u> of the four photographs or other color reproductions of your work that you have brought with you. DO NOT DISCUSS THE SAME WORK IN BOTH QUESTIONS. DO NOT DISCUSS WORKS FROM THE SAME MEDIUM IN BOTH QUESTIONS. If, for example, you have brought two reproductions of sculptures and two reproductions of paintings, you must answer one question with reference to one of the sculptures, and the other question with reference to one of the paintings. Read both Question 3 and Question 4 before deciding which of your works you will discuss in each.

When you turn in the test materials at the end of the testing period, staple the reproductions of the works about which you wrote to the pages indicated.

Question 3
(Suggested time—25 minutes)

The following question consists of two parts and is to be answered with reference to one of the reproductions of your work that you have brought with you. Using appropriate art vocabulary, write your answer to Question 3 on pages 82–85. You may incorporate diagrams, sketches, etc., in your response. Be sure to staple the reproduction of the work you are discussing in Question 3 to page 81.

Before beginning your response, you may wish to make notes or an outline in the space provided on the next page. Your notes will not be used in scoring your response. As you write your response, be careful to write the response to PART A in the section of the test book labeled PART A, etc. Answer each part of the question completely. Generally, two full pages have been allotted for each part of the question, although it is not necessarily the case that all parts of the question require responses of equal length.

From the four examples of your work that you have brought with you, select the one that best represents your strength(s) as an artist. Discuss the work you have chosen with regard to the following:

Part A

- Identify the elements of art and principles of composition that are dominant in this work. Analyze the role they play in the expression or construction of meaning. Why did you choose to emphasize them?

Part B

- Are the subject, problem, and/or medium of this work typical of your other work? If yes, why? If no, why not? What motivated you to undertake this work?

Begin your response on page 82.

(Question 3—*Continued*)

Write your response to **Question 3** on the lined pages provided.

Before beginning your response, you may wish to make notes or an outline in the space provided below. Your notes will not be used in scoring your response.

BEFORE YOU TURN IN THE TEST MATERIALS, STAPLE THE REPRODUCTION OF THE WORK DISCUSSED IN QUESTION 3 TO THIS PAGE SO THAT IT FITS INSIDE THE TEST BOOK.

Notes

STAPLE THE REPRODUCTION HERE.

Begin your response to Question 3 here.

Please provide the following information:

- Title of work: _____

- Date of completion: _____

- Dimensions of work: height _____ width _____ depth _____

- Medium or media: _____

- Other relevant physical characteristics (if any): _____

Part A

- Identify the elements of art and principles of composition that are dominant in this work. Analyze the role they play in the expression or construction of meaning. Why did you choose to emphasize them?

_____

_____

_____

_____

_____

_____

_____

_____

_____

_____

_____

_____

_____

_____

_____

_____

(Question 3, Part A—*Continued*)

_____

_____

_____

_____

_____

_____

_____

_____

_____

_____

_____

_____

_____

_____

_____

_____

_____

_____

_____

_____

_____

_____

_____

_____

_____

_____

_____

(Question 3—*Continued*)

Part B

■ Are the subject, problem, and/or medium of this work typical of your other work? If yes, why? If no, why not? What motivated you to undertake this work?

_____

_____

_____

_____

_____

_____

_____

_____

_____

_____

_____

_____

_____

_____

_____

_____

_____

_____

_____

_____

(Question 3, Part B—*Continued*)

_____

_____

_____

_____

_____

_____

_____

_____

_____

_____

_____

_____

_____

_____

_____

_____

_____

_____

_____

_____

_____

_____

_____

_____

_____

_____

_____

_____

Question 4
(Suggested time—25 minutes)

Using appropriate art vocabulary, write your answer to Question 4 on pages 88–93. You may incorporate diagrams, sketches, etc., in your response. Be sure to staple the reproduction of the work you are discussing in Question 4 on page 87.

Before beginning your response, you may wish to make notes or an outline in the space provided on the next page. Your notes will **not** be used in scoring your response. As you write your response, be careful to write the response to PART A in the section of the test book labeled PART A, etc. Answer each part of the question completely. Generally, two full pages have been allotted for each part of the question, although it is not necessarily the case that all parts of the question require responses of equal length.

The following question consists of three parts and is to be answered with reference to one of the remaining reproductions of your work. Choose a work in a medium other than the medium in which the work you discussed in Question 3 was created. Discuss the work you have chosen with regard to the following:

Part A

- What do you consider to be the most important expressive characteristic(s) of this work?

Part B

- What do you consider to be the most important technical aspect(s) of this work?

Part C

- How does this work fit into your development as an artist? In your answer include reference to the role this work played in your philosophical and stylistic development.

Begin your response on page 88.

(Question 4—*Continued*)

Write your response to **Question 4** on the lined pages provided.

Before beginning your response, you may wish to make notes or an outline in the space provided below. Your notes will not be used in scoring your response.

BEFORE YOU TURN IN THE TEST MATERIALS, STAPLE THE REPRODUCTION OF THE WORK DISCUSSED IN QUESTION 4 TO THIS PAGE SO THAT IT FITS INSIDE THE TEST BOOK.

Notes

STAPLE THE REPRODUCTION HERE.

Begin your response to Question 4 here.

Please provide the following information:

- Title of work: _____
- Date of completion: _____
- Dimensions of work: height _____ width _____ depth _____
- Medium or media: _____
- Other relevant physical characteristics (if any): _____

Part A

- What do you consider to be the most important expressive characteristic(s) of this work?

_____

_____

_____

_____

_____

_____

_____

_____

_____

_____

_____

_____

_____

_____

_____

_____

_____

_____

(Question 4, Part A—*Continued*)

_____

_____

_____

_____

_____

_____

_____

_____

_____

_____

_____

_____

_____

_____

_____

_____

_____

_____

_____

_____

_____

_____

_____

(Question 4—*Continued*)

Part B

■ What do you consider to be the most important technical aspect(s) of this work?

_____

_____

_____

_____

_____

_____

_____

_____

_____

_____

_____

_____

_____

_____

_____

_____

_____

_____

_____

_____

_____

(Question 4, Part B—*Continued*)

_____
_____
_____
_____
_____
_____
_____
_____
_____
_____
_____
_____
_____
_____
_____
_____
_____
_____
_____
_____
_____
_____
_____
_____

(Question 4—*Continued*)

Part C

■ How does this work fit into your development as an artist? In your answer, include reference to the role this work played in your philosophical and stylistic development.

_____

_____

_____

_____

_____

_____

_____

_____

_____

_____

_____

_____

_____

_____

_____

_____

_____

_____

_____

(Question 4, Part C—*Continued*)

_____

_____

_____

_____

_____

_____

_____

_____

_____

_____

_____

_____

_____

_____

_____

_____

_____

_____

_____

_____

Chapter 10

Sample Responses to the *Art Making* Questions and How
They Were Scored

▶   ▶   ▶   ▶   ▶   ▶   ▶   ▶   ▶   ▶   ▶   ▶

This chapter presents actual sample responses to the practice questions in chapter 9 and explanations for the scores they received.

As discussed in chapter 8, there are two 5-minute questions and two 25-minute questions on the *Art Making* test. The 5-minute questions are scored on a scale from 0 to 3. The 25-minute questions are scored on a scale of 0 to 5. The general scoring guide used to score the 5-minute questions is printed below, and the general scoring guide for the 25-minute questions is printed on page 102–103. In addition to the general scoring guides, a question-specific scoring guide, which is based on the general scoring guide but is tailored to the content of each particular question, is used in scoring.

General Scoring Guide for the 5-Minute Exercises

Score	Comment

3
- Shows full understanding of the issues and concepts presented by the question
- Provides sufficient, appropriate, and accurate details or examples to support and amplify general statements
- Discusses all parts of the question appropriately; response shows superior organization, clarity, focus, and cohesiveness
- Makes insightful observations about textual and/or visual materials presented in the question; thoroughly analyzes relational issues when these are implied in the question
- Uses an extensive art vocabulary that is accurate and appropriate

2
- Shows basic understanding of the issues and concepts presented by the question
- Provides appropriate details or examples to support and amplify general statements
- Discusses the major parts of the question adequately; response shows acceptable organization, clarity, focus, and cohesiveness
- Makes accurate observations about textual and/or visual materials presented in the question; clearly analyzes relational issues when these are implied in the question
- Uses an adequate art vocabulary that is accurate and appropriate

1
- Shows little or no understanding of the issues and concepts presented by the question
- Provides inappropriate details or no details or examples to support and amplify general statements
- Ignores major parts of the question; response is unfocused, lacks cohesion, and exhibits serious flaws in communication skills
- Makes illogical or inappropriate observations about textual and/or visual materials presented in the question; misses many relational issues when these are implied in the question
- Uses incorrect or no art terminology

0
- Blank or off-topic response

Question 1—Sample Responses

We will now look at two scored responses to Question 1 and see comments from the scoring leader about why each response received the score it did.

Sample Response That Received a Score of 3 (out of possible 3)

Part A

> FORM: Form is the volume something has. The depth and dimension. Sculpture is pure form while 2D work mainly suggests form.
>
> CONTRAST: Contrast is opposing elements in a work such as black and white. It could also be opposing textures like smooth and rough placed next to each other.
>
> NEGATIVE SPACE: Negative space is all the area surrounding an object.

Part B

> Form would be used to give a painting depth and dimension. It lets the viewer believe the object can be held and felt. An artist can use contrast to emphasize something or create a feeling in an area or to make something look smoother he might add roughness all around it. Negative space is very important to creating a successful composition. It becomes a shape as well as the object it surrounds. This is used to balance the composition.

Commentary on Sample Response That Received a Score of 3

This response demonstrates full understanding of the topic. It is evident from the clarity of the response that the test taker has a thorough grasp of the information. Both parts of the question have been answered in an accurate, concise manner. Therefore, this response received a score of 3.

Sample Response That Received a Score of 2 (out of possible 3)

Part A

> FORM: an element of art, form describes what is intended by shape. Shape describes specific outlines of forms. A form is not a specific shape, though. It can be implied.
>
> CONTRAST: Similar to meaning "opposite," contrast describes a difference between two elements. For example: the contrast between light and dark images is quite noticeable. Can also describe feelings which emerge from or within an artwork.

NEGATIVE SPACE: Refers to space utilized with dark, black areas to help indicate space and dimension. Working in conjunction with positive space, black and white is juxtaposed to indicate depth or an object or form.

Part B

Painters or sculptors may use form, contrast and negative space to indicate objects or people as subjects. The addition of lines, shapes and color may help strengthen the artist's intention or design.

Commentary on Sample Response That Received a Score of 2

This response demonstrates a basic understanding of the topic. While the test taker clearly does show an awareness of the terms, there are significant weaknesses in the answer. In Part A, the terms are not clearly defined and contain inaccuracies. The definitions are also blended together with examples. Providing descriptions in place of true definitions is a less effective means of demonstrating the type of knowledge that this question is testing. The response to Part B is a general answer that needs more support to be complete. The remaining sections of the response do not compensate enough for these weaknesses to earn a higher score. Therefore, it received a score of 2.

Question 2—Sample Responses

We will now look at two scored responses to Question 2 and see comments from the scoring leader about why each response received the score it did.

Sample Response That Received a Score of 2 (out of possible 3)

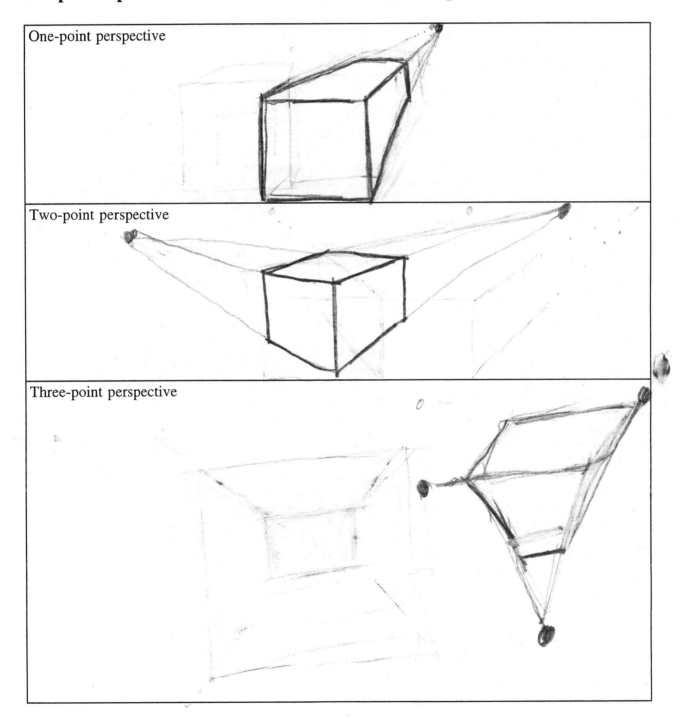

One-point perspective

Two-point perspective

Three-point perspective

Commentary on Sample Response That Received a Score of 2

In this example the test taker has accurately drawn one- and two-point perspective but has not drawn three-point perspective correctly. There are three points drawn in the bottom rectangle, but the shape of the object within them is not an accurate rendering of three-point perspective. The test taker has demonstrated "basic," rather than "full," understanding. Therefore, this response received a score of 2.

Sample Response That Received a Score of 1 (out of possible 3)

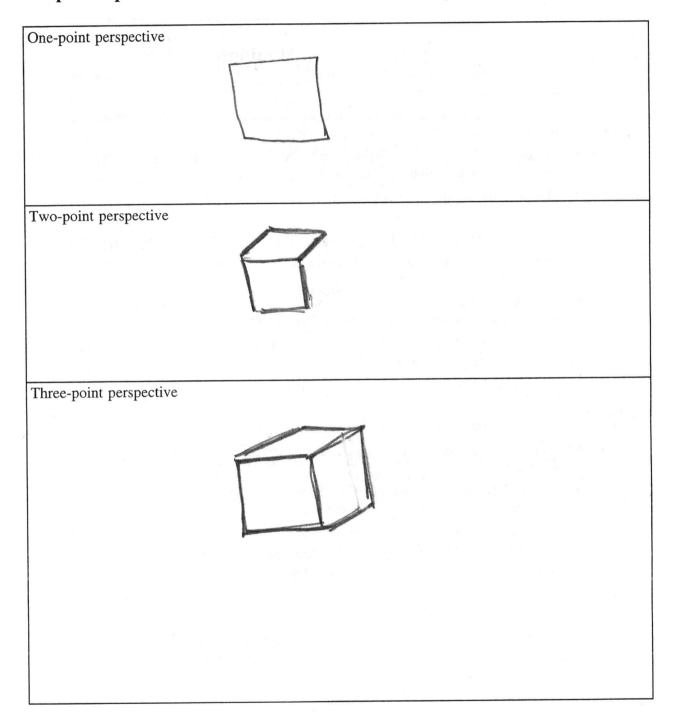

One-point perspective

Two-point perspective

Three-point perspective

Commentary on Sample Response That Received a Score of 1

This example shows the test taker's confusion about how to draw the required types of perspective. There is not enough information in the drawings to demonstrate any type of perspective. The first two drawings do not represent cubes. The third is an attempt at a cube, but even this drawing does not accurately represent any of the three types of perspective required. Therefore, this response received a score of 1.

General Scoring Guide for the 25-Minute Essay Questions

Score		Comment

5
- Shows full understanding of the issues and concepts presented by the question
- Provides a sufficient number of appropriate and accurate details or examples to support and amplify general statements
- Discusses all parts of the question thoroughly; response shows superior organization, clarity, focus, and cohesiveness
- Makes in-depth, insightful observations about his or her work; thoroughly analyzes relational issues when these are implied in the question
- Uses an extensive art vocabulary that is accurate and appropriate

4
- Shows substantial understanding of the issues and concepts presented by the question
- Provides appropriate and accurate details or examples to support and amplify general statements
- Discusses the major parts of the question thoroughly; response shows good organization, clarity, focus, and cohesiveness
- Makes in-depth observations about his or her work; clearly analyzes relational issues when these are implied in the question
- Uses art vocabulary appropriately and accurately

3
- Shows basic understanding of the significant issues and concepts presented by the question
- Provides basically correct and appropriate details or examples to support and amplify general statements
- Discusses the major parts of the question adequately; response shows acceptable organization, clarity, focus, and cohesiveness
- Makes accurate or appropriate observations about his or her work; adequately analyzes relational issues when these are implied in the question
- In most cases, uses art vocabulary appropriately and accurately

Score		Comment

2
- Shows limited understanding of the issues and concepts presented by the question
- Provides some inappropriate details or no details or examples to support and amplify general statements
- Discusses the major parts of the question inadequately or in a limited manner; response shows weak organization, lacks clarity, focus, and cohesiveness, and exhibits flaws in communication skills
- Makes some illogical or inappropriate observations about his or her work; misses many relational issues when these are implied in the question
- Uses some art terms inaccurately

1
- Show little or no understanding of the issues and concepts presented by the question
- Provides inappropriate details or no details or examples to support and amplify general statements
- Ignores major parts of the question; response is unfocused, lacks cohesion, and exhibits serious flaws in communication skills
- Makes illogical or inappropriate observations about his or her work; misses many relational issues when these are implied in the question
- Uses incorrect or no art terminology

0
- Blank or off-topic response

Question 3—Sample Responses

We will now look at two scored responses to Question 3 and see comments from the scoring leader about why each response received the score it did.

Sample Response That Received a Score of 4 (out of possible 5)

> Refer to appendix C, page 179 for an image of the artwork for this response.

Part A

When analyzing this color reduction wood cut I believe one of its most dominant principle of design is the use of balance. Due to my fascination and study of the architecture of both Romanesque and Gothic cathedrals, I feel it important to show this formal balance in my own design of the stained glass window. I created a vertical central axis that divides the window in two equal parts which is common in both paintings and religious stained glass windows. There is unity throughout the composition due to the fact that color has been reduced to 2 major hues. Red and Blue are the prominent color used traditionally in stained glass windows. I simplified my color pallet to these colors to simplify my design. The yellow was used to symbolize light as well as the use of a cream paper. The use of line helps to create rhythm throughout the piece. The contours throughout the body (representative of the leading in windows) help to give an almost static stability to the many other free-flowing contour lines.

Part B

Subject

The subject of stained glass windows and religious imagery is something that I had not previously visited in my own art production. I have, however, focused in my study of the history of religious art in the Romanesque period. I do focus quite often in my own work on architectural subject matter, be it buildings, cityscapes, etc. I chose for this print to take an architectural element, such as a window and focus on the details from a Cathedral.

Problem

> When analyzing this work, I reflect on the difficulty I had to portray the richness in the colors. I am so amazed by the vibrant colors you can see in stained glass, that I was frustrated at my inability to achieve those same rich colors. I tend to work monochromatically quite often with subtle use of vibrant colors, but at this point I wanted something bright and fresh and I struggled with that. I was working with a birch plywood, which at times tended to split with the grain and fight my curved lines.

Medium

> The medium and process of color-reduction wood-cut prints is very common to me. I love the physical nature of woodcuts and I feel that color-reduction is the most challenging both mentally and physically. In this work, like most reduction prints, you must not anticipate an exact result. The inks tend to layer differently with every image. Color selection was quite tricky, but I feel the result was successful.

Motivation

> I wanted to continue my use of architecture in my printmaking, but felt I needed to shift in a new direction. My study of the Chartres Cathedral gave me a new excitement for the aesthetic quality of stained glass. I felt I could be challenged by attempting a color-reduction print of my own stained glass window.

Commentary on Sample Response That Received a Score of 4

This response flows smoothly and logically from a well-informed discussion of the principles of composition—"balance," "unity," and "rhythm"—to the elements and how they are developed: "The use of line helped to create rhythm throughout the piece." The response is thorough and includes frequent use of appropriate art vocabulary. Discussion of subject, problem, medium, and motivation are all plausible, consistent, and connected to the description of elements/principles. The only weakness in this essay is the lack of a strong analysis of the role that the elements and principles play in expression and construction of meaning. For this reason the response earned a score of 4 rather than 5.

Sample Response That Received a Score of 3 (out of possible 5)

> Refer to appendix C, page 180 for an image of the artwork for this response.

Part A

> In this work of art the dominant elements are line, texture, and color. The print was originally just an etching of the words and trees with sugar lift for the leaves of the tree. I printed a few prints from that then aquatinted the plate to show textures for grass and to make paths. I emphasized the line to etch in the part of my favorite poem by Robert Frost at the bottom. Then I created the scene that I saw in my mind while thinking about the poem. The texture in the leaves and grass are to make it appear more realistic. The color was added to the "Woods Revisited" to create the feeling of fall in the woods which is a beautiful time of year.

Part B

> This piece is not really typical of my artwork because I do no have access to a printing press. This piece was done for class. I was motivated to do this work because of my favorite poem by Robert Frost. I took a line from the poem that I believe is true for everyone. Life revolves around your life choices and that is how I got to where I am today. Because of this I wanted to make a print expressing it.
>
> I created other prints using different techniques and I enjoyed printmaking with zinc plates. If I had access to the material needed to create more prints and more plates it would be more typical of my artwork.

Commentary on Sample Response That Received a Score of 3

This response is brief and descriptive and provides a basic answer to the question. Part A briefly discusses three elements: "line, texture, and color." There is no mention of or reference to the principles of composition. The construction of meaning is addressed superficially: "Then I created the scene I saw in my mind while thinking about the poem." Meaning is not directly tied to the elements of art or principles of composition. There is an adequate explanation of topic and motivation: "I was motivated to do this work because of my favorite poem by Robert Frost." Although the response is accurate, it stays at a relatively superficial level. Therefore, it received a score of 3.

Question 4—Sample Responses

We will now look at two scored responses to Question 4 and see comments from the scoring leader about why each response received the score it did.

Sample Response That Received a Score of 3 (out of possible 5)

> Refer to appendix C, page 181 for an image of the artwork for this response.

Part A

The Dancers are incised on the body of the porcelain vase are the most expressive. The dance each one to its one drummer. The rhythm of movement is emphasized by the background being carved out. The celadon glaze pools in the incised areas adding a darker edge to the figures. The flowers that are carved on the neck express a feminity. The form of the vase compliments the dancers & is very feminine.

Part B

The most important technical aspects were the materials: porcelain and the glaze: celadon.

Porcelain is hard to carve out because it is difficult to tell when it changes from leather-hard to bone dry — often it just snaps. This was a high fire porcelain and it is difficult to reach that firing cone 10 without under or over firing it.

The glaze is a reduction glaze and the kiln needed to be shut off to reach the shade of green achieved here.

So I had to be able to wheel throw the piece, trim it, carve or incise the pattern and the fire the kiln to cone 10 @ 2300°F in a reduction atmosphere without getting too much reduction (glaze develop flows) or too little reduction (celadon would be yellow-green) or getting kiln too hot (slumping the porcelain or (making glaze run onto the kiln shelf.)

Part C

> The work fits into my development as an artist because it celebrates women — which much of my art is about. They are united and in a circle that makes them strong but just like the porcelain of the vase they are fragile. The movement of the figures is very consistent with the way I use line in my painting. There is a rhythm that is expressed in each dancers movements. The flowers give the viewer a place on the vase to let their eyes rest. There is a suggestion on pattern (2 flowers above the dancers) with a verticle bar coming from the rim dividing the flowers) but the pattern is slightly different in each segment. This is something I constantly do in my paintings as well — I set up a pattern but then it morphs into something else — such as life.

Commentary on Sample Response That Received a Score of 3

In Part A, this essay provides a basic explanation of the most important expressive characteristics of the work. Part B, dealing with the technical aspects, is much stronger and more complete. There is an elaborate description of the process of working with porcelain from constructing to decorating and finally firing the piece. In the final part of the question, there is a nice analogy: "They [women] are united and in a circle that makes them strong but just like the porcelain of the vase they are fragile." There is weakness in the explanation of the role of the piece in the philosophical and stylistic development of the artist. It consists mainly of a description of the piece. In summary, the response includes some strong parts, combined with others that are more superficial. This response demonstrates a basic understanding of the question and, therefore, received a score of 3.

Sample Response That Received a Score of 2 (out of possible 5)

Refer to appendix C, page 182 for an image of the artwork for this response.

Part A

The most important characteristic of *Journey to Italy*, is the story it tells about a trip to Italy. It is significant because it is a chronological time line that uses words taken from the journal kept while travelling in Italy. My time in Italy is a life changing event. The way to express this event is to create a piece that expresses my thoughts and feelings. The viewer can read this piece and know my feelings.

Part B

The most important technical aspect of this work is creating words that are both contexually and graphically appealing. Once the image of Italy is in place and the colors are applied I must problem away to make the words appeal to the viewer. This means that the colors, placement and style of the handwriting affects the entire piece.

Part C

Journey to Italy demonstrates my development as an artist. This work is an example of how my trip to Italy changed me artistically. During my time there I was able to explore new media and expand my artistic skills. It allowed me to take risks.

Commentary on Sample Response That Received a Score of 2

This response indicates a lack of understanding of the question. Instead of an explanation of the expressive characteristics of the work, there is a comment that the "viewer can read this piece and know my feelings." The essence of the question remains unanswered. The technical aspects are vague and confusing: "Once the image of Italy is in place and the colors are applied I must problem away to make the words appeal to the viewer." The last part of the response is also problematic. In answer to the role the work played in philosophical and stylistic development, the test taker writes, "During my time there I was able to explore new media and expand my artistic skills." This response is unfocused and incomplete in the sense that it does not directly address the questions asked. Therefore, it received a score of 2.

Chapter 11

Preparing for the *Art: Content, Traditions, Aesthetics, and Criticism* **Test**

▶   ▶   ▶   ▶   ▶   ▶   ▶   ▶   ▶   ▶   ▶   ▶

The goal of this chapter is to provide you with strategies for how to read, analyze, and understand the questions on the *Art: Content, Traditions, Aesthetics, and Criticism* test and then how to outline and write successful responses to the questions.

Introduction to the Test

The *Art: Content, Traditions, Aesthetics, and Criticism* test is intended primarily for people who are completing teacher education programs and who plan to become teachers of art. The test is composed of three 20-minute constructed-response questions that measure the test taker's ability to analyze and discuss artworks, including architecture, in terms of content, meaning, and historical context and to discuss and apply art criticism to artworks. Test takers have typically completed a bachelor's degree program in art or art education.

The first type of question, on the content of artworks, requires the test taker to analyze and discuss how aspects of an artwork, such as style, composition, and so on, are related to the content of the artwork. The essay question may also ask about the purpose or intent of an artwork.

The second type of question, on traditions in art, architecture, and design, requires the test taker to recognize the historical context of artworks and to discuss the artworks with reference to the

- role of the artist in society
- stylistic and thematic influences of artists, architects, and movements on one another
- stylistic and thematic relationships between art, architecture, and culture within one or more periods
- transmission of cultural values through two- and three-dimensional images and forms

The third type of question, on art criticism and aesthetics, requires the test taker to do one or more of the following:

- demonstrate knowledge of basic principles of art criticism and aesthetics and apply that knowledge to describe, analyze, interpret, evaluate, judge, and critique artworks
- read, interpret, and evaluate art criticism as part of the process of applying that criticism to artworks
- interpret meaning in art as expressed through the narrative content, imagery, symbolism, and emotional effect of artworks

What to Study

Success on this test is in part a matter of learning more about how to respond to constructed-response questions. But it also takes real knowledge of the field. As mentioned above, the test is designed to gather evidence about your knowledge and your ability to analyze and discuss artworks, including architecture, in terms of their content, meaning, and historical context and to discuss and apply art criticism to artworks.

This test assumes that you have studied art during your college career, whether through a survey of art history course, through art history incorporated into other courses, or through more in-depth or specialized course work. The questions are all designed to focus on aspects of art that it is reasonable to expect a beginning art teacher to know about. Some questions do require identification of important works, but the primary focus is on using your knowledge of art and art history and criticism to think about and analyze the works that the questions refer to. Each essay question will be accompanied by reproductions of one or two works of art. You are not expected to have an encyclopedic knowledge of art history, criticism, and aesthetics. It is likely that at least some of the questions you may be asked to respond to will be based on works that you are not familiar with in depth. In these cases, your general knowledge of art history, aesthetics, and criticism should enable you to respond to the specific questions you are asked.

To prepare for the test, you may want to review books and notes in the areas of the content of artworks, traditions in art, architecture, and design, and art criticism and aesthetics.

The following books, periodicals, and Web sites are particularly relevant to the types of knowledge and ability covered by the test.

Note: The test is not based on these resources, and they do not necessarily cover every topic that may be included on the test. Similarly, these resources cover a much broader range of topics than could ever be represented in a single test.

Books

Atkins, Robert. *ArtSpeak: A Guide to Contemporary Ideas, Movements and Buzzwords*. Abbeville Press, 1990.
    A book of essays and timeline of Post WWII art and art criticism.

Barasch, Moshe. *Language of Art*. New York University Press, 1997.
    This book discusses how the communicative function of a work of art can be thought of as a language beyond its iconographic elements.

Barasch, Moshe. *Theories of Art: From Plato to Winckelmann, Vol I*.
Barasch, Moshe. *Theories of Art: From Winckelmann to Baudelaire, Vol II*.
Barasch, Moshe. *Theories of Art: From Impressionism to Kandinsky, Vol III*. New York University Press, 1985.
    This is a three-volume series on art theory that offers comprehensive analysis of major trends in art theory and branches out into several disciplines, including art history, art criticism and abstract aesthetics.

Barnet, Sylvan. *A Short Guide to Writing About Art*. Longman, 2002.
    Included in this book about the approaches to writing about art are several sample essays accompanied by analysis.

Clarke, Michael. *The Concise Oxford Dictionary of Art Terms*. Oxford University Press, 2001.
    Written by the Director of the National Gallery of Scotland; more than 1,800 entries cover periods, styles, materials, techniques, and foreign terms.

Fichner-Rathus, Lois. *Understanding Art*. 5th ed., Harcourt, 1998.
    By looking at key terms, movements, and artists, this book provides a comparative view of visual art.

Gilbert, Rita. *Living with Art*. 5th ed. McGraw-Hill, 1998.
    Art appreciation text with a comprehensive discussion of the themes, purposes, and elements of art.

Kleiner, Fred S. and Christin J. Mamiya. *Gardner's Art Through the Ages*. Wadsworth, 2005.
    This classic text moves the reader through the history of art and includes numerous chapters on art beyond the Western tradition.

Lauer, David. *Design Basics*. 6th ed., Wadsworth, 2004.
    This book illustrates what design is/should be through visual examples from different time periods and various cultures.

Lazzari, Margaret, and Dona Schleiser. *Exploring Art: A Global Approach*. Thomson Learning, 2002.
    This book uses an interesting approach to artworks in multiple contexts and provides links from one section of the book to another for further insights.

Poore, Henry. *Composition in Art*. Dover, 1991.
    This book demonstrates the principles of composition through analysis of works from the Middle Ages to the present.

Stokstad, Marilyn. *Art History*. Pearson Publications, 2004.
    This comprehensive book provides a very clear narrative, looking at many facets of art in and beyond the Western tradition, as well as "The Artist Speaks" sections that provide insights into particular objects.

Sturken, Marita. *Practices of Looking: An Introduction to Visual Culture*. Oxford University Press, 2001.
    This book explores the visual analysis of painting, photography, and new media.

Taylor, Joshua. *Learning to Look: A Handbook for the Visual Arts,* University of Chicago Press, 1981.

Wilkins, David G., Bernard Schultz, and Katheryn M. Linduff. *Art Past, Art Present*. 4th ed., Prentice-Hall, 2001.
    This book looks at the history of art both in and beyond the Western tradition, exploring the history of visual imagery through theme, technique, and relationships of past art with present art.

Periodicals

Art Times, published monthly, includes editorials, reviews, artist profiles, and art criticism.
    PO Box 730, Mt. Marion, NY 12456-0730

Art News, published monthly, includes artist profiles, museum-exhibition news and reviews, and news and inside reports on events and issues that shape the art world.
    48 West 38th Street, New York, NY 10018

Art in America, published monthly, creates a fascinating picture of the art world—the colorful and often controversial art scene here and abroad.
    575 Broadway, Fifth Floor, New York, NY 10012

ArtForum, published 10 times per year, includes features, news, reviews, and editorials.
    350 Seventh Ave, NY, NY 10001

Web Sites

www.artlex.com
   ArtLex is an online dictionary of visual art that focuses on aesthetics, along with art production, art history, art criticism, and art education.

www.aesthetics-online.org
   This is the official Web site of the American Society for Aesthetics.

All major museums also maintain Web sites related to their collections, which can be very useful. Searching on the name of the museum will provide links to its Web site.

Understanding What the Questions Are Asking

To write a successful response to a question, the first and most important factor is to understand the question thoroughly. Often, test takers jump into their written responses without taking enough time to analyze exactly what the question is asking, how many different parts of the question need to be addressed, and how the information in the accompanying artwork or quotes needs to be addressed. The time you invest in making sure you understand what the question is asking will very likely pay off in a better performance, as long as you budget your time well. Ideally, you want to use enough of your time reading the question to make sure that you do understand it, but not so much that you are left with too little time for writing. Examine the overall question closely; then identify what specific questions are being asked, mentally organize your response, and outline your key themes. Thinking out your response beforehand will help you organize your thoughts, and your response will probably be stronger.

Sample Question

To illustrate the importance of understanding the question before you begin writing, let's start with a sample question:

Audrey Flack's *Queen* is an example of Photorealism, an art movement of the 1970s that grew out of a revival of interest in realism. Write a critique of this work in which you discuss the following:

Part A

What are the primary concerns and techniques of Photorealism as represented by Queen?

Part B

How does Flack's treatment of realism compare with the treatment of realism in earlier periods, for example, Dutch Realism or nineteenth-century Realism?

Part C

How does the work challenge the viewer's perception of reality and art? Why is it challenging? What questions does the work cause the viewer to ask?

Identifying the Key Components of the Question

There are three parts to the question.

- For Part A, you are asked to describe Photorealism, using *Queen* as an example.

- For Part B, the first thing you have to do is to select at least one additional example of realism to write about; the two that are given can be used, or you can pick your own example or examples.

- Once you have chosen at least one earlier example of realism for Part B, you have to compare that style with Flack's realism.

- For Part C, you have to explain the work's impact in terms of the specific questions that are asked.

Organizing Your Response

Successful responses start with successful planning, either with an outline or with another form of notes. By planning your response, you greatly decrease the chances that you will forget to answer any part of the question. You increase the chances of creating a well-organized response, which is something the scorers look for. Your note-taking space also gives you a place to jot down thoughts whenever you think of them—for example, when you have an idea about one part of the question while you are writing your response to another part. Like taking time to make sure you understand what the question is asking, planning your response is time well invested, although you must keep track of the time so that you leave enough time to write your response.

To illustrate a possible strategy for planning a response, focus again on the sample question introduced in the previous section. You might begin by jotting down the three parts of the question on your notes page, leaving space under each. This will help to ensure that you address each part when you begin writing.

Sample Notes—Main Parts to be Answered

Here you start by identifying each part of the question:

A. Photorealism defined

B. Comparison of Flack's realism with earlier realism

C. Impact on viewer, challenge, question

You then might quickly fill out the main ideas you want to address in each part. Let's assume that for Part B, you want to discuss both forms of realism that are given as examples. You might start to fill in your notes like this:

Sample Notes—Ideas Under Each Main Part

A. Photorealism defined
  — Recreate look of photographs
  — Create painting from photographs

B. Comparison of Flack's realism with earlier realism
    — Dutch still lives
    — Discuss lighting, composition
    — 19th-century Realism
    — Discuss subject matter

C. Impact on viewer, challenges, questions
    — Perception of reality
    — What is art?
    — Validity in forms of expression

To earn the highest number of points from the scorers, you will need to do all of the following:

- Answer all parts of the question.

- Give reasons for your answers.

- Demonstrate knowledge of the subject in your answer.

- Refer to the given artwork or stimulus (quotes, etc.).

Now look at your notes and add any ideas that would address these characteristics. Notice below the additions that have been made to outline the sample response that follows the notes.

Sample Notes—With Added Ideas

A. Photorealism defined
    — Recreate look of photographs
        Photorealism is a movement in which artists sought to recreate the look of
            photographs
        Use example of D. Eddy's New Shoes, took photograph and turned it into an oil
            painting
        Seems too realistic to be a painting
        Include feminist symbolism

B. Comparison of Flack v. various art periods
    — Dutch still lives
        17th-century Dutch still lives, realistic portrayal but maintained look of a
            painting
    — Discuss lighting, composition, subject matter
        Flack's use of lighting is more realistic
        In the composition, objects overflow the boundary, seems as if you are
            looking at the real thing
    — 19th-century Realism
        19th-century Realism portrayed life as it occurred, not as it exactly looked

— Discuss subject matter
  Realistic subject matter (surgery, social injustice) used—refer to Eakins
    and Daumier

C. Impact on viewer, challenges, questions
  — Perception of reality
    Difficulty in determining if the scene is real or created
  — What is art?
    This work is not "grand manner," landscape or portrait—refer to critics
  — Validity in forms of expression
    Valid form of expression like photography, pop art or op art

You have now created the skeleton of your written response.

Writing Your Response

Of course, the information provided in the notes in the box on the previous page is not at all comprehensive. The test taker might have chosen to include other information. For example, in Part A, a test taker could also talk about how many Photorealists, including Flack, have worked by projecting slides onto their canvases. Or, in Part B, the test taker might have mentioned that the nineteenth-century Realists, such as Courbet, were among the first artists to make use of photography, then a new form of technology, to support their work. The possibilities are wide ranging.

Now the important step of writing your response begins. The scorers will not consider your notes when they score your paper, so it is crucial that you integrate all the important ideas from your notes into your actual written response.

Some test takers believe that every written response on a Praxis test has to be in formal essay form—that is, with an introductory paragraph, then paragraphs with the response to the question, then a concluding paragraph. This is the case for very few Praxis tests (e.g., *English* and *Writing*). The *Art: Content, Traditions, Aesthetics, and Criticism* test does **not** require formal essays, so you should use techniques that allow you to communicate information efficiently and clearly. For example, you can use bulleted or numbered lists, or a chart, or a combination of essay and chart.

Returning to the sample question, you can see below how the outline of the response to the question can become the final written response. What follows is an actual response by a test taker.

Part A

Audrey Flack's *Queen* is an example of photorealism which is a movement in which artists sought to recreate photographs or the look of photographs. For example, D. Eddy did a work entitled *New Shoes* in which he took a photograph and turned it into an oil painting. It is difficult to tell the difference between the two. *Queen* has the look of a photograph also. It seems too realistic to be a painting. This work is a mass of feminist symbolism—including the *Queen* chess piece—very powerful, and fruit symbolizing fertility, sensuality.

Part B

Flack's treatment of realism is very different from realism of earlier periods. For example, she does not use the look of the Dutch still lives of the 17th century. Those paintings were realistic portrayals of bowls of fruit, wine, etc, But still maintained the look of an oil painting. Flack uses a much more realistic lighting uses a much different composition. She allows the objects in *Queen* to overflow their boundary. It seems as if you are looking at the real thing. She is also quite different from the realism of the 19th century. Artists like Eakins and Daumier were more interested in using realistic subject matter, like surgery or a social injustice. They did not attempt to portray life exactly as it looked, but as it occurred.

Part C

Flack's work challenges the perception of reality and art in many ways. It is difficult to determine if the scene is real or created, for one thing. Also, this type of work goes against those critics who believe art must be landscape, portrait, etc. This is not a "grand manner" work. Can a painting that looks like a photo be art? Of course it can. It is no different than accepting photography, pop art or op art as valid forms of expression. The tight line used in this type of work takes talent to recreate.

In Conclusion

Whatever format you select, the important thing is that your answer be thorough, complete, and detailed. You need to be certain to do the following:

- Answer all parts of the question.
- Give reasons for your answers.
- Demonstrate knowledge of the subject in your answer.
- Refer to the given artwork and/or stimulus (quotes, etc.).

It is a good idea to use the practice test in the next chapter to help develop a plan for how you will take the test on the actual testing day, especially if you tend to get nervous or "freeze up" in a testing situation. Whatever format you select for your essay, the important thing is that your answer be thorough, complete, and detailed.

Chapter 12

Practice Questions—*Art: Content, Traditions, Aesthetics, and Criticism*

► ► ► ► ► ► ► ► ► ► ► ►

Now that you have studied the content topics and have worked through strategies relating to constructed-response questions, you should answer the following practice questions. You will probably find it helpful to simulate actual testing conditions, giving yourself 60 minutes to work on the questions. You can cut out and use the answer sheet provided if you wish.

Keep in mind that the test you take at an actual administration will have different questions, although the proportion of questions in each area and major subarea will be approximately the same. You should not expect your responses to these practice questions to be at exactly the same level as when you take the test at an actual administration, because numerous factors affect a person's performance in any given testing situation.

When you have finished the practice questions, you can score your answers and read the explanations for the scores the responses received in chapter 13.

THE **PRAXIS**
S E R I E S
Professional Assessments for Beginning Teachers ®

TEST NAME:

Art: Content, Traditions, Aesthetics, and Criticism

3 Practice Questions

Time—60 Minutes

Question 1
(Suggested time—20 minutes)

Question 1 refers to the two works reproduced on page 183 in appendix C.

Image 1: Polychrome Jar. A.D. 600–1150.

Image 2: Peter Voulkos. *El Pili.* 1990.

The two pieces shown on page 183 were produced several hundred years apart, one in a pre-Columbian culture, the other in the United States in the twentieth century. Write an essay in three parts in which you do the following:

Part A: Briefly discuss the surface treatment of the two pieces. Include a discussion of the roles played by the motifs, patterns, or surface decorations you identify in <u>each</u> piece.

Part B: Briefly compare and contrast the two pieces. In your discussion, focus on an element or feature found in both works that might reflect a difference in the way the two cultures view ONE of the following:

- the nature of beauty and art

- the role of art in the culture that produced it

Part C: Briefly discuss the possible utilitarian, decorative, or ceremonial functions, as appropriate, of each of the two pieces.

Write your response to **Question 1** on the lined pages provided.

Before beginning your response, you may wish to make notes or an outline in the space provided below. Your notes will <u>not</u> be used in scoring your response. As you write your response, be careful to write the response to PART A in the section of the test book labeled PART A, etc. Answer each part of the question completely. Generally, two full pages have been allotted for each part of the question, although it is not necessarily the case that all parts of the question require responses of equal length.

Notes

Begin your response to Question 1 here.

Part A: Briefly discuss the surface treatment of the two pieces. Include a discussion of the roles played by the motifs, patterns, or surface decorations you identify in <u>each</u> piece.

_____

_____

_____

_____

_____

_____

_____

_____

_____

_____

_____

_____

_____

_____

_____

_____

_____

_____

_____

_____

_____

_____

(Question 1, Part A—*Continued*)

_____

_____

_____

_____

_____

_____

_____

_____

_____

_____

_____

_____

_____

_____

_____

_____

_____

_____

_____

_____

_____

_____

_____

_____

(Question 1—*Continued*)

Part B: Briefly compare and contrast the two pieces. In your discussion, focus on an element or feature found in both works that might reflect a difference in the way the two cultures view ONE of the following:

■ the nature of beauty and art

■ the role of art in the culture that produced it

_____

_____

_____

_____

_____

_____

_____

_____

_____

_____

_____

_____

_____

_____

_____

_____

_____

_____

_____

(Question 1, Part B—*Continued*)

_____

_____

_____

_____

_____

_____

_____

_____

_____

_____

_____

_____

_____

_____

_____

_____

_____

_____

_____

_____

_____

_____

_____

_____

_____

_____

(Question 1—*Continued*)

Part C: Briefly discuss the possible utilitarian, decorative, or ceremonial functions, as appropriate, of each of the two pieces.

_____

_____

_____

_____

_____

_____

_____

_____

_____

_____

_____

_____

_____

_____

_____

_____

_____

_____

_____

_____

(Question 1, Part C—*Continued*)

_____

_____

_____

_____

_____

_____

_____

_____

_____

_____

_____

_____

_____

_____

_____

_____

_____

_____

_____

_____

_____

_____

_____

_____

_____

Question 2
(Suggested time—20 minutes)

Question 2 refers to the work reproduced on page 184 in appendix C and the quote reproduced below.

Georgia Mills Jessup. *Downtown.* 1967.

In *Progress in Art*, Suzy Gablik writes that she does not see the history of art as a succession of individual styles that are largely independent of their cultural context. Rather, she suggests that the history of art is a reflection of the ongoing but changing relationship between human beings and the political, social, economic, and natural environments in which they live. She goes on to argue that the changes in this ongoing relationship have led to changes in the way in which artists in particular and human beings in general understand and represent the world.

Write an essay in two parts in which you do the following:

Part A: Briefly state whether you agree or disagree with Gablik's view of art as an integrated whole, or a system that reflects the political, social, economic, and natural environments that are part of human experience. Explain why you agree or disagree with Gablik's view.

Part B: Briefly discuss Jessup's painting and the way it represents late-twentieth-century urban experience in terms of either Gablik's view of the history of art or your own view.

Write your response to **Question 2** on the lined pages provided.

Before beginning your response, you may wish to make notes or an outline in the space provided below. Your notes will <u>not</u> be used in scoring your response. As you write your response, be careful to write the response to PART A in the section of the test booklet labeled PART A, etc. Answer each part of the question completely. Generally, two full pages have been allotted for each part of the question, although it is not necessarily the case that all parts of the question require responses of equal length.

Notes

Begin your response to Question 2 here.

Part A: Briefly state whether you agree or disagree with Gablik's view of art as an integrated whole, or a system that reflects the political, social, economic, and natural environments that are part of human experience. Explain why you agree or disagree with Gablik's view.

_____

_____

_____

_____

_____

_____

_____

_____

_____

_____

_____

_____

_____

_____

_____

_____

_____

_____

_____

_____

(Question 2, Part A—*Continued*)

_____

_____

_____

_____

_____

_____

_____

_____

_____

_____

_____

_____

_____

_____

_____

_____

_____

_____

_____

_____

_____

_____

_____

_____

(Question 2—*Continued*)

Part B: Briefly discuss Jessup's painting and the way it represents late-twentieth-century urban experience in terms of either Gablik's view of the history of art or your own view.

_____

_____

_____

_____

_____

_____

_____

_____

_____

_____

_____

_____

_____

_____

_____

_____

_____

_____

_____

_____

_____

(Question 2, Part B—*Continued*)

Question 3
(Suggested time—20 minutes)

Question 3 refers to the work reproduced on page 185 in appendix C.

> Duane Hanson. *The Tourists*. 1970.

The Tourists reflects the revival of interest in realism that arose in the 1970's and came to be known in sculpture as Superrealism. Briefly discuss the sculpture with reference to the following:

Part A: What do you think is the meaning of *The Tourists*? Why do you think Superrealism was chosen as an appropriate style for communicating that message?

Part B: How does the style affect the viewer's experience of the work?

Part C: What are some of the aesthetic and philosophical questions that the work presents to the viewer? How might a viewer respond to those questions?

Write your response to **Question 3** on the lined pages provided.

Before beginning your response, you may wish to make notes or an outline in the space provided below. Your notes will not be used in scoring your response. As you write your response, be careful to write the response to PART A in the section of the test booklet labeled PART A, etc. Answer each part of the question completely. Generally, two full pages have been allotted for each part of the question, although it is not necessarily the case that all parts of the question require responses of equal length.

Notes

Begin your response to Question 3 here.

Part A: What do you think is the meaning of *The Tourists*? Why do you think Superrealism was chosen as an appropriate style for communicating that message?

_____

_____

_____

_____

_____

_____

_____

_____

_____

_____

_____

_____

_____

_____

_____

_____

_____

_____

_____

(Question 3, Part A—*Continued*)

_____

_____

_____

_____

_____

_____

_____

_____

_____

_____

_____

_____

_____

_____

_____

_____

_____

_____

_____

_____

_____

_____

_____

_____

_____

(Question 3—*Continued*)

Part B: How does the style affect the viewer's experience of the work?

_____

_____

_____

_____

_____

_____

_____

_____

_____

_____

_____

_____

_____

_____

_____

_____

_____

_____

_____

_____

(Question 3, Part B—*Continued*)

(Question 3—*Continued*)

Part C: What are some of the aesthetic and philosophical questions that the work presents to the viewer? How might a viewer respond to those questions?

_____

_____

_____

_____

_____

_____

_____

_____

_____

_____

_____

_____

_____

_____

_____

_____

_____

_____

_____

_____

_____

_____

(Question 3, Part C—*Continued*)

_____

_____

_____

_____

_____

_____

_____

_____

_____

_____

_____

_____

_____

_____

_____

_____

_____

_____

_____

_____

_____

_____

_____

_____

_____

No Test
Material

Chapter 13

Sample Responses to the *Art: Content, Traditions, Aesthetics, and Criticism* Questions and How They Were Scored

► ► ► ► ► ► ► ► ► ► ► ►

This chapter presents actual sample responses to the practice questions in chapter 12 and explanations for the scores they received.

As discussed in chapter 7, each question on the *Art: Content, Traditions, Aesthetics, and Criticism* test is scored on a scale from 0 to 5. The general scoring guide used to score these questions is reprinted here for your convenience. In addition, a question-specific scoring guide, which is based on this guide but tailored to the content of each particular question, is used in scoring.

General Scoring Guide for the 20-Minute Essay Questions

<u>Score</u>	<u>Comment</u>
5	■ Shows full understanding of the issues and concepts presented by the question
	■ Provides a sufficient number of appropriate and accurate details or examples to support and amplify general statements
	■ Discusses all parts of the question thoroughly; response is clear and focused throughout
	■ Makes in-depth, insightful observations about textual and/or visual materials presented in the question; thoroughly analyzes relational issues when these are implied in the question
	■ Uses an extensive art vocabulary that is accurate and appropriate
4	■ Shows substantial understanding of the issues and concepts presented by the question
	■ Provides appropriate and accurate details or examples to support and amplify general statements
	■ Discusses the major parts of the question thoroughly; response is generally clear and focused
	■ Makes in-depth observations about textual and/or visual materials presented in the question; clearly analyzes relational issues when these are implied in the question
	■ Uses art vocabulary appropriately and accurately
3	■ Shows basic understanding of the significant issues and concepts presented by the question
	■ Provides basically correct and appropriate details or examples to support and amplify general statements
	■ Discusses the major parts of the question adequately; response is inconsistent with respect to clarity and/or focus
	■ Makes accurate or appropriate observations about textual and/or visual materials presented in the question; adequately analyzes relational issues when these are implied in the question
	■ In most cases, uses art vocabulary appropriately and accurately

Score		Comment

2
- Shows limited understanding of the issues and concepts presented by the question
- Provides some inappropriate details or no details or examples to support and amplify general statements
- Discusses the major parts of the question inadequately or in a limited manner; most of the response lacks clarity and/or focus
- Makes some illogical or inappropriate observations about textual and/or visual materials presented in the question; misses many relational issues when these are implied in the question
- Uses some art terms accurately

1
- Shows little or no understanding of the issues and concepts presented by the question
- Provides inappropriate details or no details or examples to support and amplify general statements
- Ignores major parts of the question; response is consistently unfocused and/or unclear
- Makes illogical or inappropriate observations about textual and/or visual materials presented in the question; misses many relational issues when these are implied in the question
- Uses incorrect or no art terminology

0
- Blank or off-topic response

Question 1—Sample Responses

We will now look at three scored responses to Question 1 and see comments from the scoring leader about why each response received the score it did.

Sample Response That Received a Score of 4 (out of possible 5)

Part A

> The surface of the pre-Columbian piece is decorated with a painting or glazing technique. The paint could be an under glaze or over glaze, or it could be a coloring oxide or stain, or it could be another type of pigment or paint. The motifs and patterns used in the pieces are varied. The register or band above the face has a motif similar to the Greek key design. This adds structure and order to the piece. Above this band are some organic plant like motifs that are placed in a repetitive pattern. This may symbolize growth or fertility. Below the Greek key like register, is a mask like form. Facial features are painted on the face as design motifs. This may represent a tribe or a spiritual leader, or a ritualistic way that the people of this culture painted their faces. It could even be a deity of some sort. Below the face is a painted design of squares and dots that repeat themselves. The colors used in this piece are repeated throughout the whole surface decoration, unifying the piece.
>
> The surface decoration of the Voulkos piece is very different than that of the pre-Columbian piece. First of all, the wood firing technique creates a surface decoration of its own. Wood firing leaves charred surfaces and ash deposits on clay forms, giving it a more rustic, antique finish. The artist also altered the piece subtly creating an irregular surface that lends to the piece's look of antiquity the artist made marks and textural impressions on the clay surface that age the piece. The piece almost looks like it has eroded over time.

Part B

> The role of art in each color was most likely very different. In pre-Columbian civilization the function of art was probably ceremonial and utilitarian. While at the same time decoration and visual expression of culture, ritual, and belief was an important part of art. In other words, art served as functional and decorative. The form is fluted at the top to make it suitable as a container of some sort, and colorful paint and motifs were used to decorate the form.

The role of art in modern day America is quite different than in pre-Columbia. Today, artists and art collectors are more interested in form, idea, and aesthetics, more than function and decoration. The Voulkos piece embodies these new concepts. It is not a functional form and does not employ the use of highly decorative technique. Instead, its aesthetic form and appearance is achieved through subtle altering, a few carefully chosen impressions, and natural occurrences in the firing process.

Part C

The pre-Columbian piece may have served as a utilitarian container to carry water, grain, or corn meal. This piece may also have served as a decorative piece in someone's dwelling or as a dowry in a wedding. The piece may also have a ceremonial function such as a funerary urn, or may have been used in religious rituals.

The Voulkos piece is not a utilitarian piece. It has some aspects of a ceremonial piece. Its asymmetry and rough textural finish remind one of the Japanese tea bowls used in tea ceremony. The Voulkos piece may also serve as an aesthetic decoration for someone's home. One may just enjoy looking at it for what it is.

Commentary on Sample Response That Received a Score of 4

The response is analytical and thoughtful, and it goes beyond simple descriptions. It demonstrates the test taker's prior knowledge and ability to interpret the functions and roles of each of these objects accurately within the context of their culture and time: "In pre-Columbian civilization the function of art was probably ceremonial and utilitarian. While at the same time decoration and visual expression of culture, ritual, and belief was an important part of art."

The response makes connections that integrate the similarities in and the differences between the two examples into a reasoned and logical interpretation. The major parts of the question are discussed thoroughly, and statements are supported with details and examples. It is worth noting that there are several errors in the writing that appear to be matters of writing rather than substantive mistakes; for example, "The role of art in each color was most likely very different." (Instead of "color," probably "culture" was intended.) Test takers are given the benefit of the doubt, as long as the intended meaning can be deduced, and the response is not graded down. This response, therefore, received a score of 4.

Sample Response That Received a Score of 3 (out of possible 5)

Part A

> Polychrome jar was painted after it was fired and the images are of nature animals & plants. Using a broad band near the top including a geometric design repetitive and possibly religious in meaning. Bottom jar has a head built onto the jar and painted it looks like the image painted there is of a pyramid made of blocks each with two spots in it. The head is at the top of this pyramid.
>
> El Pili the method of firing produced much of what we see as surface treatments here. Wood firing in a stack produces burned markings, and lends an abstract feeling to the work. It doesn't look glazed or if so just a simple neutral one.

Part B

> These two pieces are very different as are the cultures that produced them. The Poly jar was obviously created with great care and is quite functional as a receptacle. The other probably wouldn't hold liquid, and is probably not intended to be used but to be viewed as art in its own right. The Polychrome jar was probably meant to hold grain or food of some kind. Perhaps as an offering to the gods, or to their leader. Great care went into creating beautiful images of their world nature, animals, and their god (head) on the Poly jar. The Peter Voulkos work has no function. Its existence is its function. The unique shape and burned texture sets it apart.
>
> The Peruvian culture used art to celebrate their gods and their world around them.
>
> Our culture uses art to celebrate itself.

Part C

> The Polychrome jar has a handle of sorts with the chin of the built-on head on the side. This jar may have been carried on the head with one hand reaching up to steady the load by holding the chin of the head image/shape. Probably carried food or firewood, though the ornate and detailed decorations, painted after firing, as well as the weight of a ceramic this size preclude carrying it very far. Probably ceremonial for their gods or religious or political leaders.

> Peter Voulkos piece Bigger, more massive piece, with heavy base – you could probably break in a door with it, but just once This work probably is meant to be put on display, and had no other utilitarian purpose. Decorated minimal, and the only ceremonial function being with celebration of art.

Commentary on Sample Response That Received a Score of 3

This response is relatively brief but accurate. Each of the three parts of the question is addressed succinctly. Little attempt is made to elaborate on cultural connections or to integrate the roles of the surface decoration of each piece. The answers are descriptive rather than insightful: "Bottom jar has a head built onto the jar and painted it looks like the image painted there is of a pyramid made of blocks each with two spots in it. The head is at the top of this pyramid." A very basic interpretation is given for the functional nature of the objects. This is an excellent example of a response that meets the requirements and criteria for a basic score of 3.

Sample Response That Received a Score of 2 (out of possible 5)

Part A

> The the surface of the first piece is smooth and glaced compared to the second piece which has a unfinished texture. The first piece has been colored and coated with ceramic glaze but the second piece is fired but not coated.
>
> The decoration done on the first piece is more prominent by the patterns and motifs. The top part is the representation of vegetation and plants which must be an influence of nature. A protruding part represents a face. It suggests that face painting was a common tradition and reflects a cultural aspect of people.
>
> The surface of the second piece is rough. The carving is done to show the important of sculptural art. Artist's intention is to preserve this work by firing the piece.

Part B

> If you compare both pieces with each other, their purpose seem to be the same, jars must have been used for storing liquids or drinking wine. The artist of the first piece is more towards the visual beauty for a common person, whereas the second one must have executed for distinct appreciator of art. The art style of the first one could be found in every house, but the second one, though in distorted condition, must be amongst the collection of high class patronage.

> The nature has been converted in color and shape visually in the first piece, where as in the second piece the concept of nature has been taken. For example animal figures have been carved. The shape is more important than the color.
>
> The role of art is prevailing in both the cultures which produced them. The first one shows that common people executed art in their daily life. In the second piece, the decoration is done for art sake. In the second culture art is more important than the usefulness.

Part C

> The first one could be used for storing and drinking wine especially on special occasions.
>
> The second piece could be barely decorative but in some occasion could be used for liquid as a server.

Commentary on Sample Response That Received a Score of 2

This response shows incomplete understanding of the complexity of the question. The statements are often inaccurate (e.g., the test taker writes that the "second piece could be barely decorative but in some occasion could be used for liquid as a server," which is clearly implausible because of the openings in the vessel) and provide incomplete or limited information. Although the quality of writing is not scored in and of itself, this is an example of a response in which the confusion about the content seems to be reflected in writing that is also confusing and difficult to read. The response demonstrates only a limited ability to analyze and interpret the two objects, and the response is incomplete. Therefore, it received a score of 2.

Question 2—Sample Responses

We will now look at three scored responses to Question 2 and see comments from the scoring leader about why each response received the score it did.

Sample Response That Received a Score of 5 (out of possible 5)

Part A

> It is interesting that you have chosen Gablik's quote as a subject I have always had a difficult time in school studying straight history whether U.S., Eurpean or World. It was not until my first Art History survey course in college many years ago (courtesy of Mr. Janson & his tome) that the names, dates, wars and movements finally clicked into place. (In fact, I wonder that the somewhat far-apart art movements of the mid to late 20th century, such as expressionism, Dadaism, Pop Art & conceptual art,

will show us as a society with no direction, going every different way and briefly adoring every new work, the more outrageous, the better.)

From the earliest recorded history, art has not only reflected what was going on, but also the role of the artist in that society. Egyptian, Greek & Roman art have shown the ideal, the real and the overblown, and the developmental trend can also be traced from the pre-Renaissance anatomy developments of Giotto then the genius of Michelangelo to the overblown and tortuous writings of Bernini and the Rococco decorators.

There are tides of reaction, opposition, replacement, rest, and then the circle begins again. (Why, one may ask, with all of the wonderful and "correct" anatomy of the Greeks and Romans surrounding them, did the 3rd century artists of Constantini produce short, stubby, ungraceful and "unattractive" [to our eyes] sculptures. The answer is: precisely as a reaction to the wonderful monumental and what the Christians regarded as representative of their persecutors and Roman paganism. The figure in sculpture can be seen to have grown from this first phase, through to the stylized and elongated figures we see in the 12th century catherdrals of Vezelay, Moissac and Autun. It even takes a side trip to Germany to foreshadow expressionism (i.e., the tortured writhing figures of Christ in). And so on, until the realism came around again during the late Gothic period in 14-15 century France. [I could write volumes more – this is a subject of great interest to me, but time does not permit.]

Part B

Jessup's painting of downtown (New York) is a perfect reflection of our times: so much is going on there are signs, traffic lights, bridges, vehicles, marques, some trees, and all tightly packed together and jostling for attention. So much so, that some things are fuzzy and out of focus. One does not know where to look first.

And her people crowded tightly at the ground, and surrounded by all this activity all separated from each other by black lines and indistinct as well none recognizable, just a part of the scene. Certainly a statement of how I feel when I'm in New York. Who can argue that minimalism as a reaction to this painting, at least, is a refreshing breather.

The movements in art now, in this jet-age world of ours resemble a three-ring circus see it all at once, anything you want, anything goes. One wonders what the next step in development can be, when we seem to "have it all".

Commentary on Sample Response That Received a Score of 5

This test taker articulates a strong response, rich with insight and thoughtful commentary. There is passion in these words, based on knowledge of the subject. It is a compelling answer. The analysis of the Jessup painting is convincing and eloquent. It meshes with the Gablik statement and makes a profound observation of the power of art in the late twentieth century: "The movements in art now, in this jet-age world of ours resemble a three-ring circus see it all at once, anything you want, anything goes. One wonders what the next step in development can be, when we seem to 'have it all'." The response demonstrates a thorough understanding of the question and, therefore, earned a score of 5.

Sample Response That Received a Score of 3 (out of possible 5)

Part A

> I agree with Gablik's statement that art is a "system" that reflects the political, social, economic, and natural environments that are part of human experience. Art is the expression of all these things by different people at different times. Occasionally artists claim to do work that is very personal, and not influenced by others. This might be true from their perspective but what is very personal to them is a compilation of everything they have experienced in their lifetime. With each change in one's environment, their frame of reference is altered. This is clearly evident in viewing the different styles one single artist may work with in his or her life.

Part B

> Downtown is an effective expression of the late 20th century urban experience. Anyone in "Any Downtown, USA" can identify with the painting. The bright colors, cluttery busy atmosphere all convey "Downtown". When taken under the influence of Gablik's view of art history one can say that Jessup is reporting the urban environment as it exsists to her and her time. I see a strong cubist influence in the work and this can be discussed in terms of Gablik's statement as well. Any successful artist has studied cubism, therefore, it has permeated their frame of reference. The inclusion of cubist ideas is merely a supporting element for Gablik's theory of art history.

Commentary on Sample Response That Received a Score of 3

This response shows a solid, basic understanding of the question. The test taker has taken a point of view on the statement and provided brief evidence to support it: "Occasionally artists claim to do work that is very personal, and not influenced by others. This might be true from their perspective but what is very personal to them is a compilation of everything they have experienced in their lifetime."

The connection between the Gablik statement and the Jessup painting is accurate, simple, and authentic. There is adequate organization and focus within the body of the response to indicate an understanding of the concept as it was presented. Therefore, the response received a score of 3.

Sample Response That Received a Score of 2 (out of possible 5)

Part A

> Throughout art history all changes in art styles are due to social and political changes. Expressions resulted from the desire of artists to break away from traditional ways of viewing life around them and the succession of art that has followed has always reflexed social change. Some of these changes were brought on by a society at war. The artist attempts to visualize the horrors of war, such as the artist Bacon did.
>
> The on set of the industrial revolution brought about cubism and pop art was caused by a tongue-in-cheek look at our society.

Part B

> Jessup's painting of "Downtown" is a just what Gablik describes about the changes in society and how it reflects the outlook of the artisians. The painting, done in aesthetic cubism, reveals the break in realistically drawn landscapes.
>
> She has chosen to paint her view of urban life in the twentieth-century with lights and signs and the geometric patterns that are reflected in our modern citys and typical of cubism.

Commentary on Sample Response That Received a Score of 2

In this response there is some attempt to address the questions posed, but it is quite limited. The answer strays from the topic and demonstrates an incomplete understanding of what was asked: "Expressions resulted from the desire of artists to break away from traditional ways of viewing life around them and the succession of art that has followed has always reflexed social change." No position is actually taken in opposition or agreement with the Gablik statement. The answer is incomplete and confused and does not connect Gablik's point of view of the history of art with Jessup's painting in a clear or substantive way. Therefore, the response received a score of 2.

Question 3—Sample Responses

We will now look at three scored responses to Question 3 and see comments from the scoring leader about why each response received the score it did.

Sample Response That Received a Score of 5 (out of possible 5)

Part A

> I think the meaning of *The Tourists* is it is like a mirror. The viewer, once he or she figures out this is, indeed, a sculpture, are forced to ask themselves "This is Art?" The confrontation between the viewers and their pre conceived notions about art and beauty is where I believe the meaning of this piece lies. I think superrealism was an extremely appropriate style for communication that message. It is better, much better, than its metaphoric mirror because it unsettles the viewer in the thought.

Part B

> The viewer is unsettled by supperrealism. A guy walks by and wonders what these "tourists" are looking at. He looks up and sees nothing. He looks back and they are still staring. "Oh, they are statues". He smiles and chuckles, then maybe checks out how the artist made them look so real. Probably later in the day, or that night he starts to wondering. Why is that art? Those people were not beautiful. What do I look like when I think no one is watching? Is anyone watching?
>
> I think supperealism sets this sort of swirling inner debate among viewers.

Part C

> "What, exactly, is art?" "Well art makes ya think". "Does art need to be beautiful?" "Well it ought to be, but after seein' this, I reckon not." "Does that mean I am art?" "Yes I am."
>
> I think this work displays the subject/object paradox in art wonderfully. The reason it is wonderful is it does it with humor in a non threatening way. It's all about the art object and the way we as individuals relate to it subjectively. My reaction to this would be dramatically different than my grandmother & I imagine my 5 year old daughter's would blow both of ours away. The point is art is your relationship with it.

Commentary on Sample Response That Received a Score of 5

Original analysis of meaning and experience highlight this superior response: "The confrontation between the viewers and their pre conceived notions about art and beauty is where I believe the meaning of this piece lies." Read holistically, the response flows smoothly from one part of the question to the next, relating all the essential aspects of the material together in a unified position statement.

Although this response is not particularly long, the aesthetic issues raised by the subject and style are thoroughly questioned and discussed in a logical, insightful, and methodical fashion, the trademark of superior responses: "I think this work displays the subject/object paradox in art wonderfully. The reason it is wonderful is it does it with humor in a non threatening way. It's all about the art object and the way we as individuals relate to it subjectively." Therefore, the response received a score of 5.

Sample Response That Received a Score of 3 (out of possible 5)

Part A

> The meaning is the experience of seeing, being, and experiencing the tourists. We have all been tourists. The images take us back remind us of our vacation.
> Superrealism was chosen because it expresses the experience in 3 dimensional form. The figures become part of the environment & thus we become part of theirs. We look up to see what they are looking at and share.
> They are life size art people placed in the real world. Superealism allows them into our world and make us part of theirs.
> It creates a sharing of experience.

Part B

> The style makes us part of the work by joining their world with ours.
> The figures are so life like that we accept them as people. They could be one of us – or are they one of us? When we go to museums etc we bring our cameras and wear our weird clothes.
> Their stance pulls us into the piece and then we follow their gaze into the environment, thus mixing the 2 worlds.
> It's like a snap shot. We experience a moment frozen in time. They are Art People sharing a moment with the real people.
> They are life like and they are non threatening. They are everyday people out enjoying themselves and allowing us to enjoy them.

Part C

> Philosophically People are alike in so many ways. To me it shows that everyday people are in fact works of art.
>
> Are people plastic cut outs of each other? No but we are similar to one another. I think the viewer responds by becoming part of the piece. Memories help us share the experience. The life size figures share our world.
>
> Can art be people or people art? Yes.
>
> There will never be an answer to what is art. It's up to the opinion of the artists & viewer. To me this is great art. People shown realistically and beautifully allowed to share our environment with us.

Commentary on Sample Response That Received a Score of 3

This is a solid, basic answer. The test taker demonstrates the ability to accurately interpret the meaning of the sculpture and the appropriateness of Superrealism as a style to represent this meaning: "They are life size art people placed in the real world. Superrealism allows them into our world and make us part of theirs. It creates a sharing of experience."

In Parts B and C, the response is accurate, but it tends to be relatively superficial. Part B says relatively little about the viewer's experience and talks again about the work as a whole. The aesthetic and philosophical responses can also be characterized as basic: "Can art be people or people art? Yes." Therefore, the response received a score of 3.

Sample Response That Received a Score of 1 (out of possible 5)

Part A

> The meaning can be found in the artist desire to depict the individual as being as real as possible. In his attempt to create the average stereotyped tourist (American) the artist wishes to define a general attitude and behavior of the American culture. It is in the realm of realism that we find the stereotypical expression of the American society. The cameras express material consumption, the handbag and the clothing express the values and choices of the average social individual. The style brings the viewer into his or her own world. Its hard to distinguish who are the viewers and what is the art.

Aesthetically the viewer see him or herself and is allowed to ask questions about the beauty of everyday choices in fashion and expression. It is a reflective mirror that the viewer looks into and challenges his/ or her sense of values. When we are asked to judge our own values we ask to look inward. To examine or moral, aesthetic and spiritual selves. Do we really look like that? In this way we become more self conscience of our choices in a cultural perspective.

Part B

Style of the the

Commentary on Sample Response That Received a Score of 1

This response starts off well, and the answer to Part A of the question would possibly merit a score of 3, but Part B and Part C have been omitted. Because of the omission of Parts B and C, the response received a score of 1.

Chapter 14

Are You Ready? Last-Minute Tips

► ► ► ► ► ► ► ► ► ► ► ►

Checklist

Complete this checklist to determine whether you're ready to take the test.

- ❑ Do you know the testing requirements for your teaching field in the state(s) where you plan to teach?

- ❑ Have you followed all of the test registration procedures?

- ❑ Do you know the topics that will be covered in the test you plan to take?

- ❑ Have you reviewed any textbooks, class notes, and course readings that relate to the topics covered?

- ❑ Do you know how long the test will take and the number of questions it contains? Have you considered how you will pace your work?

- ❑ Are you familiar with the test directions and the types of questions for the test?

- ❑ Are you familiar with the recommended test-taking strategies and tips?

- ❑ Have you practiced by working through the practice test questions at a pace similar to that of an actual test?

- ❑ If you are repeating a Praxis Series assessment, have you analyzed your previous score report to determine areas where additional study and test preparation could be useful?

The day of the test

You should have ended your review a day or two before the actual test date. On the day of the test, you should

- be well rested

- take photo identification with you

- take a supply (at least three) of well-sharpened #2 pencils if you are taking a multiple-choice test

- take blue or black ink pens if you are taking a constructed-response test

- eat before you take the test to keep your energy level up

- be prepared to stand in line to check in or to wait while other test takers are being checked in

You can't control the testing situation, but you can control yourself. Stay calm. The supervisors are well trained and make every effort to provide uniform testing conditions, but don't let it bother you if the test doesn't start exactly on time. You will have the necessary amount of time once it does start.

You can think of preparing for this test as training for an athletic event. Once you've trained, prepared, and rested, give it everything you've got. Good luck.

Appendix A
Study Plan Sheet

▶ ▶ ▶ ▶ ▶ ▶ ▶ ▶ ▶ ▶ ▶ ▶

Study Plan Sheet

See Chapter 1 for suggestions about using this Study Plan Sheet.

STUDY PLAN						
Content covered on test	How well do I know the content?	What material do I have for studying this content?	What material do I need for studying this content?	Where could I find the materials I need?	Dates planned for study of content	Dates completed

Appendix B
For More Information

► ► ► ► ► ► ► ► ► ► ► ►

ETS offers additional information to assist you in preparing for The Praxis Series assessments. *Test at a Glance* materials and the *Registration Bulletin* are both available without charge from our Web site: **http://www.ets.org/praxis/index.html.**

General Inquiries

Phone: 800-772-9476 or 609-771-7395 (Monday-Friday, 8:00 A.M. to 7:45 P.M., Eastern time)

Fax: 609-771-7906

Extended Time

If you have a learning disability or if English is not your primary language, you can apply to be given more time to take your test. The *Registration Bulletin* tells you how you can qualify for extended time.

Disability Services

Phone: 800-387-8602 or 609-771-7780

Fax: 609-771-7906

TTY (for deaf or hard of hearing callers): 609-771-7714

Mailing Address

ETS—The Praxis Series
P.O. Box 6051
Princeton, NJ 08541-6051

Overnight Delivery Address

ETS—The Praxis Series
Distribution Center
225 Phillips Blvd.
Ewing, NJ 08628

Appendix C
Book of Reproductions

► ► ► ► ► ► ► ► ► ► ► ►

Chapter 5

Practice Test for *Art: Content Knowledge*

Questions 9 and 10 refer to the following.

Scala/Art Resource, NY

Question 15 refers to the following.

©Erich Lessing/Art Resource, NY

Question 26 refers to the following.

Eva Hesse, 1968. height: 48.3 to 51.4 cm; diameter: 27.9 to 32.3 cm.
The Museum of Modern Art, New York.
©Estate of Eva Hesse

Questions 32 and 33 refer to the following.

Chartres Cathedral, west facade, c. 1134–1220; south spire, c. 1160; north spire, 1507–13.
Vanni/Art Resource, NY

Question 37 refers to the following.

Andrea Mantegna, ceiling of the Camera degli Sposi, 1474. Fresco, 8'9" in diameter.
Palazzo Ducale, Mantua, Italy. ©Massimo Listri/Corbis

Questions 39 and 40 refer to the following.

Katsushika Hokusai, The Great Wave of Kanagawa, 1831. 9⅞" x 14⅝".
Réunion des Musées Nationaux/Art Resource, NY

Question 68 refers to the following.

Georges Seurat, *The Sideshow*, 1887–88. Oil on canvas, 39¼" x 59".
Metropolitan Museum of Art, NY. ©Francis G. Mayer/Corbis

Chapter 8

Preparing for the *Art Making* Constructed-Response Test

Pages 67 through 69 of chapter 8 refer to the following.

Lawn Ornament, 2004. Photograph, 9" x 6¼".

Chapter 10

Art Making Constructed-Response Test: Sample Responses and How They Were Scored

Question 3; Sample Response 1, Score of 4

Untitled, 2003. Woodcut, 20' x 12".

Question 3; Sample Response 2, Score of 3

Woods Revisited, 2002. 7" x 5".

Question 4; Sample Response 1, Score of 3

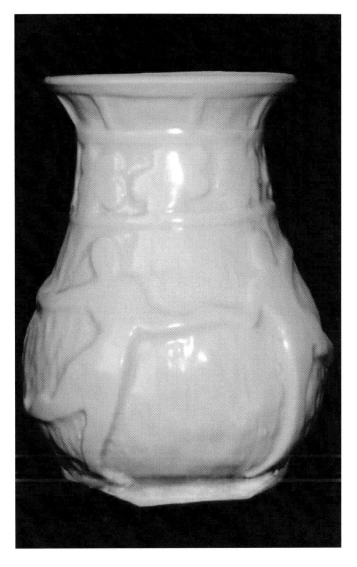

The Dance, 2001. Porcelain, 10" x 6".

Question 4; Sample Response 2; Score of 2

Journey to Italy, 2003. Oil on Canvas, 24" x 36".

Chapter 12

Practice Test for the *Art CTAC* Test

Question 1 refers to the works reproduced below.

Polychrome Jar, A.D. 600–1150. Ceramic,
24 inches high. Coastal Tiahuanco style.
Cahuachi, Rio Grande de Nazca, Peru. Photograph
by Lee Boltin, New York, New York.
Bridgeman Art Library.

Peter Voulkos, *El Pili*, 1990. Ceramic stack,
anagama fired (wood-fired), 34½" x 19½". California.
Courtesy of the Estate of Peter Voulkos and
Braunstein/Quay Gallery, San Francisco, CA.

Question 2 refers to the work reproduced below.

Georgia Mills Jessup, *Downtown*, 1967. Oil on canvas, 44" x 48".
The National Museum of Women in the Arts. Gift of Savannah Clark. Washington, D.C.
©1967, Georgia M. Jessup.